Icon Programming for Humanists

Icon Programming for Humanists

Alan D. Corré
University of Wisconsin-Milwaukee

 Prentice Hall, Englewood Cliffs, New Jersey 07632

Library of Congress Cataloging-in-Publication Data

Corré, A. D. (Alan D.)
  Icon programming for humanists / Alan D. Corré.
    p. cm.
  Includes index.
  ISBN 0-13-450180-2
    1. Icon (Computer program language) 2. Natural language
  processing (Computer science) I. Title.
  QA76.73.I19C67 1989
  055.13'3—dc20   89-32504
                                                      CIP

Editorial/production supervision: bookworks
Cover design: George Cornell
Manufacturing buyer: Mary Ann Gloriande

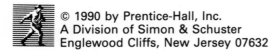

© 1990 by Prentice-Hall, Inc.
A Division of Simon & Schuster
Englewood Cliffs, New Jersey 07632

The publisher offers discounts on this book when ordered
in bulk quantities. For more information, write or call:
  Special Sales
  Prentice-Hall, Inc.
  College Technical and Reference Division
  Englewood Cliffs, NJ 07632
  (201) 592-2498

Printed in the United States of America

10 9 8 7 6 5 4 3 2 1

ISBN   0-13-450180-2

Prentice-Hall International (UK) Limited, *London*
Prentice-Hall of Australia Pty. Limited, *Sydney*
Prentice-Hall Canada Inc., *Toronto*
Prentice-Hall Hispanoamericana, S.A., *Mexico*
Prentice-Hall of India Private Limited, *New Delhi*
Prentice-Hall of Japan, Inc., *Tokyo*
Simon & Schuster Asia Pte. Ltd., *Singapore*
Editora Prentice-Hall do Brasil, Ltda., *Rio de Janeiro*

For Nita

Rabbi Judah ben Idi said in the name of Rabbi Johanan: We know from references in Scripture that the Shekina left Israel by ten stages: from the Ark-cover to the Cherub and from the Cherub to the threshold of the Holy of Holies and from the threshold to the court and from the court to the altar and from the altar to the roof of the Temple and from the roof to the wall and from the wall to the city and from the city to the mountain and from the mountain to the desert and from the desert it ascended and abode in its own place, as it is said: "I will go and return to my place." (Hosea 5.15)

Babylonian Talmud, *Rosh Hashana*, 31a.

Contents

Preface

The first rule of computer programming is: Don't learn BASIC. This is no disparagement of BASIC. In its time this language was an important contribution to bringing programming out of the control of the gurus and making it accessible to the general public, and it also anticipated the growing importance of interactive computing where the user engages in dialogue with the machine. But by nature it was a simplification of FORTRAN which had preceded important advances in the understanding of the necessity for proper structuring in programming. Just as the divine Shekina moved at a critical period in discrete steps, so the flow of a program must move in clear, distinct steps and each individual section must "return to its place." BASIC has got great mileage from its name, which appears to denote ease and simplicity. But this appearance is illusory. It is much better to learn proper, disciplined principles from the beginning, as it is in most areas of life. Being addicted to appropriate objects is perhaps the ultimate key to success.

The Icon programming language is a good choice for those whose main interest is the written word. It is structured so that it emphasizes proper programming principles, yet it does not carry the philosophy of structuring to the lengths of Pascal. It strikes a reasonable balance between structure and freedom, between being a disciplinarian like Pascal and an easygoing but perhaps overindulgent friend like SNOBOL-4, the unstructured ancestor of Icon. It has excellent facilities for handling strings of characters, which is the essence of this type of programming; flexible structures such as lists, tables, and sets; and useful built-in sort capabilities which have been further improved in the current version 7. Icon programs are quite portable. They can be written on one machine and transferred easily to another. And since Icon is in the public domain, its cost is negligible. All these features add up to making Icon the language of choice for humanistic programming.

This book teaches the principles of Icon in a very task-oriented fashion. Someone commented that if you say "Pass the salt" in correct French in an

American university you get an A. If you do the same thing in France you get the salt. There is an attempt to apply this thinking here. The emphasis is on projects which might interest the student of texts and language, and Icon features are instilled incidentally to this. Actual programs are exemplified and analyzed, since by imitation students can come to devise their own projects and programs to fulfill them. A number of the illustrations come naturally enough from the field of Stylistics which is particularly apt for computerized approaches. This book assumes an acquaintance with the concepts of elementary statistics appropriate for such work, and the reader unfamiliar with these may wish to become familiar with them first. Kenny's book referred to in the first chapter gives a clear description of these principles and may be used with profit.

A diskette in MS-DOS format is furnished with this book which contains many of the programs included in it. To use this diskette, insert it in the disk drive of an IBM or IBM compatible PC after booting the machine in the normal way. (This may require you to insert the system diskette in your machine before you switch on. Then remove it and insert the supplied diskette.) Type in

TYPE READ.ME

hit the return key, and follow the instructions. You may delay doing this until you have read the first two chapters.

My thanks are due to my friend Brooks Smith who has been of so much help in every way. I also wish to thank Eric Johnson, Chris Tenaglia, and Doug Tiarks for helpful suggestions, although they are not responsible for any errors. Last but not least, my thanks go to my wife Nita for her constant patience and support. I dedicate this work to her with much love.

A.D.C.

Icon Programming for Humanists

1
Introduction

1.1 THE ICON PROGRAMMING LANGUAGE

Why Icon? Icon is one programming language among the hundreds that have been devised so far, but is probably the best for tasks which involve the study or manipulation of natural language. Programming languages form a bridge between human beings and computers, enabling man to convey instructions to machine. Two of the earliest languages, FORTRAN and LISP, continue to be used for mathematical and artificial intelligence applications, and the great difference in character of these two languages indicated early on that there were many ways in which this man-machine communication could be carried on. In the late sixties the SNOBOL-4 language, which was deliberately designed to be different from its predecessors, appeared. Computers were originally intended to perform mathematical calculations but it became apparent that by encoding the letters of the alphabet, natural language texts could also be manipulated. SNOBOL-4 dealt primarily with strings of characters rather than numbers, and along with other original features this gave it especial power in dealing with natural language. It also had the advantage of a particularly fine manual, both in content and appearance, perhaps the best computer manual ever produced.[1] Two things have happened, however, since SNOBOL-4 appeared, one of a theoretical, one of a practical nature. First, there has been an emphasis on writing programs which are divided into smaller units systematically connected into a unified whole. This makes programs much easier to grasp for the human reader, and easier to modify subsequently. A long program which is not "structured" becomes a tangled

[1] R.E. Griswold, J.F. Poage and I.P. Polonsky, *The SNOBOL-4 Programming Language* (Englewood Cliffs, N.J.: Prentice Hall, 1971).

1

web of which it is dangerous to interfere with any strand. The popularity of the Pascal language which emphasized this approach and in fact imposed it upon its users, attests to the manner in which this notion has become accepted in the programming community. The "C" language which is widely used by professional programmers, and Ada, which has been authorized for U.S. government use, both adhere to principals of structured programming. Secondly, interactive computing, in which the user engages in dialogue with the machine, rather than furnishing it with a batch of data, has become much more common. Originally computer time and computer memory were both at a great premium. With the advent of microcomputers, affordable computing is within the reach of all. The design of SNOBOL-4 preceded these changes, and although it has been updated to take account of them, the need was felt for a language which would have features similar to SNOBOL-4, but would have a character similar to other modern, structured languages. The Icon language was evolved by Ralph Griswold and others to achieve this end. Government support was given to its development, and hence the language has the additional advantage of being in the public domain. It is available for microcomputers for a purely nominal cost, and may be found on many modern time-sharing systems.

This book aims to show how Icon can be used fruitfully in literary computing, and hence does not duplicate the standard reference on the language[2] which is an indispensable guide to using Icon. We emphasize the writing of programs which manipulate or study texts, and follow largely the kind of procedures which are mapped out for manual use in Kenny's excellent introduction to statistics for students of literature and the humanities.[3] Many of the programs developed here are in fact automations of procedures suggested by Kenny.

It is not necessary to have any previous knowledge of computers in order to be able to use this book, but you must know how to reach the operating system level of the computer you are using. If you are using a time-sharing system where several or many users employ the same machine from a different terminal, you will normally need to establish an account on the machine, and you must enquire how to do that. If you are using a microcomputer you will need to insert the system disk in the drive and start the machine. Before doing so, it is desirable to make a backup copy of your system disk, and you need to consult the directions that come with your computer for instructions how to do this. You then need to use a disk on which the full Icon system has been recorded. Be sure to get version 7, which is the version used in this book.

---

[2] Ralph E. Griswold and Madge T. Griswold, *The Icon Programming Language* (Englewood Cliffs, N.J.: Prentice Hall, 1983). This should be supplemented by Ralph E. Griswold et al., *Version 7 of Icon* (1988). This is a paper which is available from the Department of Computer Science, University of Arizona, Tucson AZ 85721.

[3] Anthony Kenny, *The Computation of Style* (Oxford, 1982).

This should similarly be protected against loss by being backed up on to a duplicate disk. It is permissible to copy the Icon system from someone else who has it, or it may be obtained for a modest fee from commercial outlets. Further details on running Icon on your machine are found in Appendix D of this book. It is suggested that you use this text in front of your keyboard, and try out the various programs that are suggested. You may experiment by making modifications and seeing what happens. This will provide a discovery procedure in learning; if you learn nothing else you will probably discover that you do not think as logically as you thought you did. To have a dialogue with the computer can be a humbling experience. Except in the rare instances where there is some hardware problem or you encounter a bug in the software the computer is excruciatingly logical.

1.2 BASIC CONCEPTS

Before we can use computers to aid us in our task we need to understand a few basic concepts. These may be divided into two sets: concepts familiar from daily life and concepts of a mathematical character. The concepts familiar from daily life are:

1. Sequence

2. Condition

3. Repetition

Let us illustrate these by reference to a cooking recipe (which is genuine but not guaranteed):

Peel vegetables.

If the beef is frozen, defrost at power 3.

Form into patties.

Layer half of patties and half of vegetables, repeat.

Microwave until vegetables are tender.

"Peel vegetables" and "Form into patties" are instructions to be carried out as they occur in the sequence of the directions. The instruction to defrost, by contrast, is dependent on the beef being frozen. If it is not, there is no need to obey the instruction, since no alternative action is specified. This illustrates the second concept, condition or choice, and it is this capacity to choose which gives the computer its great power, since it can act differently according to conditions. The last two instructions contain repetitions, often called "iteration" or "a loop." In the first case, the repetition is determined numerically, it must be done two (and not three or ten) times. It will be noted that the loop also contains a type of condition. After performing the action, if the action has been done less than twice it is repeated. If it has been done twice the repetitive act ceases. In the last action a particular condition is constantly checked. Are the vegetables tender?—no, cook some more; yes—stop cooking.

These three concepts—sequence, condition, and repetition—are all that is needed for structuring a program. The most complex operations depend on these simple ideas.

1.3 MATHEMATICAL CONCEPTS

The two concepts which are borrowed from mathematics may be a little more difficult to grasp. Let us first consider the following two statements:

> John has four children.
> John has four letters.

Both statements may be true, but in the first *John* represents a flesh-and-blood real person, whereas in the second we are speaking of the string of marks on paper or the screen. The second *John* would often be written in this context surrounded by double quote marks, and Icon uses the double quotes to surround literal strings of this kind. The first *John* is a *variable* which stands for its *value*, in this case a particular individual whose name happens to be John. In Icon any word that begins with an alphabetic letter or underscore and continues with any amount of letters, numbers, or underscores, can be a variable, provided it is not one of a small number of words which have been appropriated by Icon for special purposes. The underscore is used rather than the dash to avoid confusion with the use of the latter for subtraction and negative numbers. Thus

```
year := 1987
```

assigns the value 1987 to the variable `year`, the colon followed immediately by the equals sign being the symbol which assigns the value of what is on the right to the variable on the left. Note that from now on we shall use a script resembling that of the typewriter to represent Icon code. So

```
last_year := year - 1
```

would assign the value 1986 to the variable `last_year`, which it would retain until it is specifically altered by a new assignment. When it gets this new value, the old value is lost. It is perhaps best to regard the variable as a kind of box or container into which a value can be poured. This image is not so far from the truth, since the variable represents a location in the memory of the computer which we can more readily handle by giving it a name which we can easily remember. We mentioned that the ability of the computer to handle conditions is one of the things which gives it its great power. The ability to use variables similarly gives great power to the computer, since it makes it possible for programs to apply to a great deal of different data simply by feeding this data to a variable as appropriate. Programming rapidly becomes trivial if it cannot have a *general* program which processes *specific* data.

The other mathematical concept widely used in programming is that of the *function*. In mathematics the function establishes a connection between one set of numbers and another set. Thus the function which we call *square* associates the numbers

1, 2, 3, 4, 5...

with the numbers

1, 4, 9, 16, 25...

The function *square* applied to 2, for example, gives ("returns," "produces") 4, and 4 is the *value* of the function. In a similar manner, the Icon function **reverse()** associates the strings

```
"cram", "did", "trap", "number2"...
```

with the strings

```
"marc", "did", "part", "2rebmun"...
```

So the value of

```
reverse("cram")
```

is **"marc"**. The *function* is followed by parentheses which enclose the *argument* which is to be processed by the function. This argument may be a variable; for example

```
word := "cram"
reverse(word)
```

gives the same result. In addition to having values, functions often have *effects*. It is most important to understand this distinction. For example, the value of

```
write("cram")
```

is "cram"—but in addition this function writes the word "cram" on the screen, and directs subsequent writing to be on the next line, or, in other words, it issues a carriage return. In this instance the *effect* is normally much more significant than the value, but we shall find that the value can be used too.

A function need not always produce a result. Sometimes it does not produce anything, or to put it another way, it *fails*. As an example, the function integer() produces a whole number from its argument—if it can. The value of integer(1.5) is 1. If there is a decimal, it is simply truncated, or cut off. But integer("a") does not produce anything—it fails. There is just no way the character a can be made into a whole number. This is important, because failure is, so to say, infectious. If the result of a function that fails is passed on to another function, that function fails too, and any *effects* it may have do not occur. So if we write

```
    write(integer("a"))
```

the integer() function fails, and so write() fails too, and nothing at all happens. On the other hand

```
    write("")
```

does write a zero-length string, which is indeed nothing to speak of, but write() has succeeded, and so the effect of the carriage return will be seen in the fact that the cursor—that moving block or underline that you see on the screen—will move down. This difference between "writing nothing" (succeeding) and "not writing anything" (failing) may seem arcane or cabalistic, but it has significant results. It is one of the things that makes Icon tick. We may note in passing that write(integer("a")) is an example of a nested function: Whatever is produced by integer() is immediately passed to write().

Since we are here talking about nothing, it will be useful to refer here to some other manifestations of this strange entity, which, let us recall, is not the same as not anything. Before so doing, we may like to consider an example from English grammar which will help to explain what we are talking about. In English the plural of "horse" is "horses" and the plural of "ox" is "oxen." We can then say that to form the plural in English, we add -*s* and in a few cases which can be specified -*en*. What about "sheep"? We can say that the plural is the same as the singular. But we can *regularize* the situation by saying that "sheep" adds "-∅" which is "nothing" or, more technically, a "zero morpheme." This legal fiction is often very useful, because now *all* words add a morpheme to form the plural, and not just some, and it makes exceptional circumstances less awkward to handle. This is one of the "uses of nothing" as one linguist put it. Now we noted before that "John" is a string of four characters. We can subtract four characters from it and be left with the string of zero length which we just referred to. A function which produces a zero-length string succeeds, even though it may not seem to produce anything of great significance. This empty string is often useful however as a kind of starter to which other pieces ("substrings") may be added. The empty string is to be distinguished from the *blank* or *space*, which is a real character and has a length of one or more. Blanks are obvious when they are in between words, but is there a blank at the end of a line on the screen or a piece of paper? We shall find that the computer may sometimes want to know the answer to that question, but we can delay the answer for now. It is an historical accident that the blank is used as a word divider; some ancient scripts used a bar or some other marker that looks more like a "real" character. In addition Icon has an entity called *null*. This represents the initial value of a variable (**year** for example) before some value (such as 1987) is assigned to it. A function which produces null is in fact succeeding, even though there is not much you can do with null. The whole point of null is that it *cannot* be used in computations—whether numbers, strings of characters, or anything else is involved—since thereby if we inadvertently try to use something having that value in a computation while we are developing a program, Icon will pick it up and let us know about it by flashing an appropriate message on the screen. The notation for the null value is **&null**. The ampersand at the beginning indicates that **&null** is a *keyword*, one of several useful values which Icon specifies for us. **&null** may be used in assignments; thus if the value of the variable **year** is 1987, the command

```
year := &null
```

restores it to its initial null value. We shall find later that alternating between a null value and some other value can have distinct uses. To sum up, we must learn to distinguish *nothing at all* (which is what functions which fail produce) from a skinny motley crew consisting of the empty string, the blank (or blanks), and the null value which may be lightweights but at least they are not failures.

2
Distributions

2.1 GETTING STARTED ON A PROGRAM

This chapter will consider how Icon can be used to quantify aspects of a text. We shall do this by a simple study of word length, taking first a very brief text:

One went and came. *W.B. Yeats*

We shall then show how to expand these principles for long texts. Our task is

1. To isolate individual words.

2. To count the number of letters each has.

3. To display the numbers on the screen.

Icon possesses a line-scanning facility which is able to go through a line and process it. We invoke this facility by following our brief text with a space and a question mark thus:

`"One went and came." ?`

The text, which we shall refer to as a "string," must be between double quotes in the program because otherwise Icon would understand the words as variables. Now let us imagine that there is a pointer positioned initially at the beginning of the line immediately before the upper case *O*. This pointer indicates the point at which we are working and will gradually move through the string until our task is complete.

Icon has a function **upto( )** which will locate the position in our string immediately before *any* of the characters in its argument. Thus if we write

9

```
"One went and came." ?  upto(' .')
```

`upto()` will locate the first occurrence of a blank or a period in our string. The characters concerned, blank and period, are delineated by single quote marks. In general in Icon, the double quotes enclose a *string*—where the order of letters is significant—while single quotes enclose a *set of characters* or *cset*—where the order is irrelevant. (A *set* is a collection of items which is considered as a unity. Each item occurs once only.) At this point, the *value* of `upto(' .')` is 4, which is the position immediately before the blank. Check this by counting from position 1, which is at the beginning of the string, right before the first character ("O"). Remember that the blank or space is a character in its own right. We shall now use the Icon function `tab()`, the effect of which is to move up that imaginary pointer to the position of its argument and the value of which is the characters (in this case the first word) in between the old and new positions.

"One went and came."
    ↖   ↖
    1   4

(Positions 2 and 3 are on either side of the *n* in *One*.)
This gives us:

```
"One went and came." ?  tab(upto(' .'))
```

Since *tab* has been used, the imaginary pointer has been moved up to position 4 and we shall proceed from there. At this point the value of the expression `tab(upto(' .'))` is the string "One"— and we wish to know its length. The length of a string can be obtained in Icon simply by prefixing an asterisk:

```
"One went and came." ?  *tab(upto(' .'))
```

To check the evaluation of what follows the question mark, we must move from the innermost parentheses out – the value of `upto()` which is 4 is passed to `tab()` the value of which is "One" and the length of this is measured by the asterisk. Note that so far all this activity is purely internal to the computer; we would not be aware of what has been going on. To find out, we use the function **write** which prints out the result on the screen:

```
"One went and came." ?  write(*tab(upto(' .')))
```

Let us review what this means. We have first the string we are processing between double quotes. Then comes the question mark which means that the string will be scanned and processed by what follows. We understand what follows by considering the innermost function first. The function `upto()` returns a position in the line (of little interest to us) which is immediately fed to `tab()` which moves up the pointer (its *effect*) and produces the first word (its *value*). Observe that `tab()` has both an effect and a value. This word is turned over to the asterisk which produces its length, and finally this length is printed on the screen.

It is true that this is a lot of work to count three letters, but its power is that it can be applied generally and perform the tedious job of counting words by the hundreds. Before we do that, however, let us run this program which can tell us the length of a single word.

In Icon, programs are arranged in *procedures* which perform separate jobs and collectively make up the program. There is no absolute rule as to what should be included in a particular procedure, but arranging programs in this modular fashion greatly facilitates understanding and modification of the program at a later date. So we arrange the material we have prepared so far as follows:

```
procedure word_length()
   "One went and came." ?  write(*tab(upto(' .')))
return
end
```

Each procedure begins with the word *procedure* and is given a name we choose which must begin with a letter or underscore followed by any number of letters, numerals or underscores. It is best to give simple, descriptive names. The name is followed by the parentheses () which will be used later on to pass information to the procedure, by including between them as many variables (called arguments) as are needed to pass that information. The procedure ends with the word **end**. The indentations simply help to set off the body of the procedure from the title and the end marker, and aid visually to see the structure of the program. Later, as the procedures become more complex, further indentation will be used, rendering it always possible to see which statements belong together since they will be written at the same level of indentation. The word **return** will be followed by the final value of the procedure if it has one, and indicates that the procedure has concluded successfully, and the program flow is to return from whence it came.

One thing is left to do. Every Icon program has a main procedure which acts like a traffic cop. By looking at it we can see the skeleton structure of the program, since each procedure mentioned or "called" in the main procedure is invoked in turn. No real business should be done in the main procedure; it should simply control the flow of traffic. Since our program is quite simple, the main program will invoke only one procedure. The entire program now looks like this:

```
procedure main()
  word_length()
end

procedure word_length()
  "One went and came." ?  write(*tab(upto(' .')))
return
end
```

Procedures do not need to be in any particular order, but it is usual to place the main procedure first, since it gives a conspectus of the program to the reader. When the program is executed, it always begins with the main procedure and follows the pattern laid out there.

Let us now try to run this little program.

When you are sure that the Icon system is available on your computer, enter:

icont - -x

icont is a command to the operating system of your computer which invokes the Icon translator. This translates the program written in Icon to language which the computer can use. The first dash tells Icon to take the input from the keyboard, as you are going to type in the program. The *-x* gives an instruction to execute the program as soon as it is translated, to put it into effect immediately. Press return, and in a few moments you will see the message *Translating:* which means that Icon is ready to translate your program to a form which it can understand and run. You will then see the message *STDIN:* which is the name that Icon gives to a record of the program which it creates on disk in a form that the computer can understand. (The abbreviation stands for "standard input" which is usually the keyboard. The colon is not part of the name.)

Copy in the entire preceding program. After each procedure, Icon will tell you if you have made an error. If all is well, it will repeat the name of the procedure along with its size. If you do make a mistake, it is probably better to start over. Press *control-C* and try again. After you have finished you must type in a character to tell the system that you are finished. This depends on the system you are using. It may be a *control-D* (hold down the *ctrl* key and press *D*) or *control-Z* (which is the *F6* key on some terminals, or you may hold down the *ctrl* key and press *Z*.) You may need to press the *Return* key also. This should ultimately result in the answer: *3*. Since Icon has recorded on disk the copy of the program that the computer can read under the name *STDIN*, you can later repeat the program by typing in that word at your terminal. (On some computers you may have to precede it by the word *iconx*.)

Let us now proceed to process the rest of the line. You will remember that the imaginary pointer was positioned right after the last letter of the first word. We now have to move it over the intervening blank. Note that the blank counts as a character. The function upto(), which we have already used, gives the position immediately before any member of its argument that it finds in the string. The function many() is the converse of this; it gives the position it finds immediately after *all* members of its argument that occur consecutively after the pointer. So

```
many('.  ')
```

will skip over any periods or spaces which it finds immediately after the pointer and stop right *after* the last one. In this case the value of many(' .') is 5, which is the position after the space. If we feed this result to tab()

```
tab(many(' .'))
```

tab() will move the pointer to the point immediately after the first blank. Its value is itself a space, but this is of no interest to us and we do not use it. Since the value is not assigned to any variable, or used as the argument to any function, it is in effect discarded. tab() is used for its *effect* of moving up the pointer. However, we wish to repeat this process until the end of the line. We achieve this by inserting while in front of the write() in our program and do at the end of the line:

```
procedure main()
  word_length()
end

procedure word_length()
  "One went and came." ?  while write(*tab(upto(' .')))  do
      tab(many(' .'))
end
```

This means: *while* or *as long as* the instruction to write out a length can be carried out or *succeeds, do* what follows. Let us trace this step by step. Before we introduced this "while-loop" our pointer was positioned as follows:

"One went and came."

\ \
1 5

Icon now repeats its initial activity. It finds the next blank, gives the value *9* to tab(), moves the pointer to just before the next blank:

"One went and came."

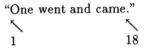

1   9

and produces the word "went". The asterisk figures its length at *4* and
write() writes it to the screen. This process continues until the pointer
reaches a point before the period:

"One went and came."

1   18

The function **many()** then produces *19* after detecting the period, and this
19 is fed to **tab()**. Now the pointer is at the end. When the next attempt to
"write" occurs, the innermost function **upto()** *fails* because **upto()** is unable
to detect a blank or a period which constitute the argument of **upto()**. The
failure is "inherited" by all the functions in a chain leading to **write()**, and
none of the failed commands is carried out. At this point the repetitive action
ceases; since the expression between **while** and **do** has failed, and since there
are no more commands, the program ends. The length of each word of the
sentence should now be on your screen.

2.2   SEPARATING DATA AND PROGRAM

So far we have been working on an extremely small text in which the text was
written right into the program. While this was a useful way to get started,
in general it is not a good idea to do this. It is better for programs to
be of general application, and to achieve this we need to leave data outside
of the program which processes the data. One way to do this is to input
the information from the keyboard, and this type of interactive computing
where the machine responds instantly is very popular nowadays. Before we
do so we have to handle one problem. We have used **upto()** to detect the
presence of a blank or a period. That was fine in the sentence "One went
and came." because each word was marked off by one or the other. But in a
continuous text many lines do not end in any particular marker, so the last
word in the line would not be noticed unless it happened to end in a period,
or someone had inadvertently typed in a space after it, which would not of
course be visible on the screen. We can easily solve this by replacing **upto()**
by **many()** and using **many()** to span all the alphabetic letters of which a
word may consist. This would necessitate writing an argument with at least
52 characters in it, but there is a simpler way. The *keyword* **&ucase** stands

for a set of *all* the uppercase (capital) letters and **&lcase** represents all the lowercase (small) letters. We can combine these sets by using a double plus sign (**++**) which is used for adding sets to each other. The single plus sign is reserved for arithmetic addition. Keeping the signs separate helps avoid programming errors. Note that elements only occur once in a set, so if you add together two sets which share certain items, the resulting set will have these items once only. Also, you can only add sets to sets; it must be in a set itself, even if that set has only one member. So

```
&lcase ++ 'Z'
```

would give you the set of the lowercase letters and uppercase *Z*. When we come to learn about sets of items other than single characters, we shall find that there is a function which can insert an item in a set. Let us now look at the modified program and consider what the differences are.

```
procedure main()
   while word_length(read())
end

procedure word_length(line)
   line ?  while write(*tab(many(&ucase ++ &lcase))) do
           tab(many('., ;:'))
return
end
```

The effect of the function **read()** is to get input from the terminal, and its value is the string which was read in from the terminal. This is passed to the procedure **word_length**. As you see, this procedure now has a variable (**line**) in its title. This variable will take the value of the argument of **word_length** and it can be used in the program. We have here an example of a perpetual loop. So long as the user inputs a line, the program will process it. In this loop the **do** is not necessary since no action takes place in the loop; it simply serves to keep on calling **procedure word_length()**. To break out of such a loop you have to enter a character provided by the operating system to terminate programs. Try *control-C* (hold down the *ctrl* key and press *C*.) When you use these so-called control characters, it is not necessary to press the shift key also.

2.3 DISTRIBUTION

So far we have simply been listing word lengths. Now we should like to do the same as before, but we shall calculate and state how many words the text has which contain one, two, three, and more letters. For this we need variables in which to store these values as we go along. It would be possible to have, let us say, ten variables, one each for one-letter words, two-letter words, and so on. It is easier however to use the *list* which is a collection of variables which all have the same name, but are distinguished by a number called an *index*. So if we call the variable `letters`, then the number of one-letter words will be stored in `letters[1]`, the number of two-letter words in `letters[2]` and so on. Notice that the index follows the name in square brackets. We can set up such a variable by entering

```
letters := list(10,0)
```

The word `list` may only be used for this purpose in Icon. It is a function the value of which is a list with as many variables as are stated in the first argument, and each has the initial value stated in the second argument. This list is assigned to a variable which you choose. So in this case, `letters` has a list assigned to it with ten values (from `[1]` to `[10]`), each of which is initially 0. The arguments are divided by commas. We chose ten because we are assuming that there will be no words of more than ten letters. If we assume the number will be higher then we must have a higher number, otherwise the longer numbers will be unaccounted for. How can we store the desired information in this list?

Previously, we did not store the length of any individual word since we wrote it out immediately. Let us use the variable `length` to store this value which we can obtain from the value of the `write()` command. At this point the program looks like this:

```
procedure main()
   while word_length(read())
end

procedure word_length(line)
   letters := list(10,0)
   line ?  while length := (write(*tab(many(&ucase ++
      &lcase)))) do
        tab(many(' .,;:!'))
   return
end
```

The third line of the procedure became long, so we broke it into two. Since it is clearly incomplete (++ expects something to follow) Icon will look for the completion on the next line. Icon considers a line to be a complete statement unless it is clearly incomplete, such as a line which ends in a "+" or similar operator, or a word like `else` which we shall find in conditional statements. All of these imply that the next line is also part of the statement. For example, the statement

```
n := 2 + 1
```

would assign the value 3 to **n**. If we wish to split the line, then

```
n := 2 +
  1
```

would have exactly the same effect. However,

```
n := 2
  + 1
```

would assign 2 and not 3 to n. Since the second line is a syntactically correct statement even though useless, it will not cause an error, but the result is not what the programmer intended, since the first line is understood by Icon as a complete statement. We now have a list called **letters**, and we have recorded the length of a word in **length**. In order to store **length** in **letters** we can write

```
letters[length] +:= 1
```

The symbols **+:=** written together mean that what is on the left is increased by the number on right, or *incremented* by that number. Now let us say the word is "a". The variable **length** will have the value *1* and so the first variable in **letters** will be incremented. If the word is "please", then the sixth variable of **letters**, i.e. **letters[6]**, will be incremented. Now this needs to be done each time we get a new word. However it is always assumed that the word **do** is followed by one and only one statement. This is covered by placing the *compound* statement inside curly brackets thus:

```
procedure main()
  while word_length(read())
end

procedure word_length(line)
  letters := list(10,0)
  line ?  while length := (write(*tab(many(&ucase ++
    &lcase)))) do {
      tab(many(' .,;:!'))
      letters[length] +:= 1}
return
end
```

At this point **letters** has all the information stored, but no use is being made of it. Now we wish to print out a table of the length of the letters in our text. It would be a good idea to put this in a separate procedure since it is conceptually a separate item. But we have a problem. When procedures finish, all the variables they use are destroyed. This is done largely to save memory. We could quickly fill up the memory of the computer with variables which we are not currently using. With the increase in the size of computer memory this is less of a problem than it used to be, but is still worth doing. We can solve this by making **letters** a *global* variable, one that can be used by all procedures in the program and does not disappear when the procedure finishes for the time being. We do this right at the beginning by prefixing the word **global**. However there is an additional problem which is a little subtle. Each time the procedure **word_length()** is called, the assignment of the list to **letters** will be done again, with the result that the old list will be destroyed. This could be handled by making this the first statement in **procedure main()**, but a better solution is simply to place the word **initial** before it which means it will only be done the first time the procedure is called and not subsequently:

```
global letters
procedure main()
   while word_length(read())
end


procedure word_length(line)
initial letters := list(10,0)
   line ?  while length := (write(*tab(many(&ucase ++
     &lcase)))) do {
       tab(many(' .,;:!'))
   letters[length] +:= 1}
return
end
```

It now remains to write a procedure to write out the table, include this procedure in the "traffic cop" main procedure and our task will be complete. Here it is:

```
global letters
procedure main()
   while word_length(read())
   printout()
end
```

```
procedure word_length(line)
initial letters := list(10,0)
  line ?  while length := (write(*tab(many(&ucase ++
    &lcase)))) do {
    tab(many(' .,;:!'))
  letters[length] +:= 1}
return
end

procedure printout()
  every n:= 1 to 10 do
    write("There are ",letters[n]," ",n,"-letter words.")
return
end
```

The explanation of **printout()** is as follows. You will recall that a while-loop functions so long as the expression following the **while** succeeds. An every-loop by contrast functions so long as the expression following it *produces a result*. It is used with Icon expressions called *generators* which can produce a group of results rather than only one. The expression 1 to 10 is such a generator, producing the whole numbers from 1 to 10, one at a time. Here n gets the values 1 to 10 in sequence. The command **write** can take any number of arguments which are separated by commas, and will be written out one after the other. So the following pattern will be written ten times:

> There are [the number of words of a specific length] [the specific length] -letter words.

For example:

> There are 4 5-letter words.

SUMMARY OF ICON FEATURES INCLUDED IN THIS CHAPTER

1. ? invokes the line-scanning facility.

2. **upto()**

   value the position in the string after the first letter found in its argument.

3. **tab()**

   value the string between the old and new positions of the pointer.

   effect moves up the pointer to the position in its argument.

4. The asterisk returns the length of the following string.

5. Each program has a *main procedure* which indicates traffic flow.

6. *icont - -x* invokes the Icon translator, expects input from the keyboard, and has the program immediately executed.

7. `many()`

   value the position in the string after all letters in its argument.

8. `write()`

   value its last argument.

   effect writes its arguments to the screen.

9. `&ucase` and `&lcase` are sets of the upper- and lowercase characters respectively.

10. `read()`

   value a string read in from the keyboard.

   effect reads in a string from the keyboard.

11. A *list* is a collection of variables that share a name and are differentiated by an index from 1 up, e.g. `letters[7]`.

12. The successful conclusion of a procedure is indicated by `return`, which is followed by the value of the whole procedure if it has one. Note that here `return` refers to a word written into a program, and not the key of that name on the keyboard.

13. A *global variable* is accessible to all procedures. It must be declared at the beginning of the program.

14. A *generator* is an expression or a function which may produce a group of results rather than one result.

15. A *while-loop* continues so long as its control statement succeeds. An *every-loop* is used with *generators*, and continues so long as the generator produces a result.

16. A command preceded by the word `initial` is done only the first time the procedure in which it occurs is used. Such commands should come at the beginning of the procedure.

3
Files

3.1 MAKING INFORMATION LAST

So far we have typed in programs from the terminal, and when data had to be input, we have typed that in too. This is satisfactory only for small programs and small amounts of data. There are two disadvantages. First, it is difficult to correct errors, either in program or data. If something goes wrong we have to do it over. Secondly, once the program is over, everything has disappeared. It is often desirable to retain both programs and data for future use. Also, they may be modified if necessary without having to start from the beginning. This is achieved by placing the program in a *file* and having it use data that is also in a file. A *file* in this context is a stream of information, and most often refers to one that has been fixed electronically onto a disk. However, the stream of information coming in from the keyboard is also technically a file, and so is the one appearing on your screen. It may be possible for you to hold the disk on which a file is registered in your hand, or it may be hidden away in a "hard" or "fixed" disk in your computer, or if you are using a time-sharing system it may be miles away and quite invisible to you. Formerly these files were often created by punching holes in cards that encoded the programs and data, and were transferred to disk by card reader machines. The most common method now is to enter the data using a keyboard and screen, and a program called an *editor* is used for this purpose. Word processors developed from these editors, but word processors are oriented towards ultimately printing the materials they handle and so possess features (word-wrap and justification, for example) which are unnecessary for editors. Many different editors are available with different capabilities, and choice is a matter of personal preference. Some word processing programs

21

may be used as editors. WORD*STAR for example, has a "nondocument mode" which can serve as an editor. The regular document mode is not suitable because it introduces special characters, invisible to the user, for its own purposes. In the following two sections some hints are given on utilizing two commonly used and readily available editors. Any can be used provided that it uses the ASCII character set referred to in Appendix A.

Editors perform two major functions:

- They place new material into a file.

- They modify or correct material which already exists.

Some editors begin by assuming that the user is editing material that already exists, and interpret whatever is typed in as commands to modify this material. The user has to give some special sign to the editor to indicate that henceforth new material is being entered. Alternatively, the editor may assume that new material is being typed in, and editing commands have to be distinguished in some way, perhaps by holding down the control key while typing them. This depends on the particular editor being used. Additionally, there are two main types of editors known as *line editors* and *full-screen editors*. The first, older, type numbers each line in the file and the user edits a single line at a time. The line is usually reached by typing in the line number. With the second, a whole screenful of text is displayed at one time, and the user moves around the screen by entering commands or using a hardware item called a *mouse* (plural: *mouses* or *mice*) to move around the screen a lighted, sometimes flashing, bar or block called the *cursor* which indicates where the user is working.

3.2   THE EDLIN EDITOR

EDLIN is an editor supplied with the operating system called *MS-DOS* or *PC-DOS* which is commonly used with microcomputers. It is a line editor which initially assumes that you are editing the file with which it is dealing. If you wish to create or edit a file called *AVERAGE.ICN*, you type in

    EDLIN AVERAGE.ICN

and press the return key. (In referring to MS-DOS files, it does not matter if you use upper- or lowercase, or mix them.) EDLIN then creates this file if it does not exist, or readies it for editing if it does. If the file is new, EDLIN will tell you that this is so, and you may then type *i* (for *insert*) and press the return key. You can then enter lines into the file, pressing the return key after each line. It is permissible to allow lines to run beyond the edge of the screen if they are long. EDLIN will indent the lines to show that they are being inserted, and number them. When you are finished, hold down the control key and press *c*. (*Control-C* is the "end-of-text" character from wireless telegraphy days.) You then make the file permanent by typing in *e* (for *end* or *exit*) and pressing the return key.

We just learned how to create a new file using EDLIN. There are many ways in which you may edit a file using EDLIN. Initially it is best to use just essential features and add new ones later. These save time rather than enabling you to do anything which could not be done with the basic features. Information on these is given in Appendix C. Much can be done with a rather limited knowledge of the real capacities of the editor, and many changes can be made in various equally good ways.

If you wish simply to view the contents of the file, press *p* (for *page*) and the return key. Repeating this action will take you through the file. When you get to the end, you may enter *1p* to repeat the process. You can in fact prefix any number to *p*, and you will be able to view a screenful of text starting at that line.

If you wish to edit a line, type in its number and that line will be presented to you and you may modify it. If you press the right arrow key on the keypad to the right of the keyboard, the characters in the line will appear one for each time that you press the key. The F1 key on the left does the same thing. If you wish to change a letter, type it in instead of pressing the arrow key, and it will replace the corresponding letter. To delete letters, press the Del key as many times as necessary, one for each letter, then continue with the arrow key. To insert characters, press the Ins key and type the letters you wish to insert. You may then continue with the arrow key. The F3 key prints the rest of the line, and by pressing return the new line replaces the old. Be careful not to press return before the line is complete, otherwise it will be truncated. It is suggested that you create a small file by copying some text, and then modify it for practice. It is important to check the manner in which the various features work, since sometimes changes are made and not fully documented. The ease with which software can be modified often causes the documentation to lag behind the way it functions. Finally, two ways of getting yourself out of trouble. If you are finished and want to abandon the editing you have done instead of saving it, type *q* (for *quit*) rather than *e*. EDLIN will ask if you really want to abort your editing session, and if you type in a *y*, will leave the original file unchanged, or just allow it to disappear if it was a new file.

3.3 THE EMACS EDITOR

EMACS is an editor meant to work with the UNIX operating system, but is not part of UNIX. (Actually it belongs to GNU. GNU stands for: "GNU'S NOT UNIX." When you ask what *that* GNU stands for, you discover that you have a definition of a type known as recursive. Remember the cereal boxes carrying a picture of a boy holding the cereal box?) It is often available on time-sharing systems, and may be copied freely, subject only to certain conditions which are stated in the documentation. EMACS is also available in a version for personal computers. EMACS is a full-screen editor which initially expects text to be inserted, and so differs from EDLIN on both counts. Accordingly you can type

   emacs average.icn

and may proceed immediately to enter your text. You should use lowercase letters on the call line. You make the file permanent by holding down the *Ctrl* key and pressing *x*, releasing the *Ctrl* key and then pressing *s* (for *save*). On some systems you may need to continue pressing *Ctrl*. (If you find that your computer "freezes" when you press *Ctrl-S*, pressing *Ctrl-Q* should get it going again.) You leave EMACS by holding down the *Ctrl* key and pressing both *x* and *c*.

   EMACS has an enormous number of features, far more than many users would ever need to use. Some of the most important will be described here. However, EMACS has a built-in tutorial which will acquaint you with the main features, and also an information tree which can be used as a reference. In order to use the tutorial, type in

   emacs

without naming a file. Then type in *Ctrl-H* (hold down the *Ctrl* key and press *h*) followed by *T*. The *Ctrl-H* summons up the "Help" facility, and *t* stands for *Tutorial*. You then simply follow instructions and are led through the main features. In some local implementations *Ctrl-H* may be replaced by something else, perhaps the *Esc* key followed by a question mark (?). You can experiment, or inquire locally.

   Here are some of the major features of EMACS. *Control-V* (for *view*) enables you to page through the file. Pressing the escape key and then *V* does the same thing in the opposite direction. It is worth pointing out that the control key modifies another key, much as the shift key does, so it must be held down while pressing the next key. The escape key, however, produces a character in its own right even though it is not normally visible on the screen, so it should be released before pressing the following key. Cursor control is achieved through *control-F* (*forward*), *control-B* (*back*), *control-P* (*previous line*), and *control-N* (*next line*). *Control-L* retypes what is currently on the screen around the current position of the cursor. This can be useful if you are using a modem and getting some noise on the telephone line which introduces characters which are not really there. Escape followed by the "less than" sign (which points back) takes you to the beginning of the file, and followed by the "greater than" sign (which points forward) takes you to the end. The delete key deletes the character immediately before the cursor, and *control-D* (for *delete*) deletes the character over the cursor. *Control-K* (for *kill*) deletes to the end of the line. This may be reversed by *control-Y* (for *yank*). This last feature may be used to move lines around the screen; kill the line, move the cursor to another place, and then yank it. The work you are doing is being held in a buffer, which is temporary storage. To make it permanent at any time press *control-X* and then *s* (for *save*).

EMACS does have automatic save features which mean that you are unlikely to lose too much work if there is some kind of breakdown involving your computer, but it is advisable to save explicitly from time to time. You can leave EMACS by pressing *control-X* and then *control-C*. Your implementation may allow you to leave EMACS temporarily (probably to try out a program) by pressing *control-Z* and then you can return to the place you were with the command *%emacs*.

These commands are sufficient to get started with EMACS. You may also wish to look at the information tree. You can do this by summoning the help facility (*control-H*, or a local substitution) and then entering *i* for *info*. Remember that you can leave EMACS at any time by *control-X control-C*.

3.4 RUNNING AN ICON PROGRAM FROM A FILE

We now have to learn how to handle a file containing a program so that the program can be run, and later how we bring data into our program which is stored on a separate file. This distinction between program and data is fundamental. In knitting we may compare the knitting pattern to the program and the yarn to the data. The yarn is manipulated on the basis of the pattern. In cooking we may compare the recipe to the program and the ingredients to the data. The ingredients are reformulated in accordance with the recipe. Formerly programs and data were kept in different types of files, but that is no longer necessary. Files containing Icon programs must end in a period and the three letters *icn*. There are differing conventions as to the format of filenames, but generally if you keep them reasonably short and stick to alphabetic and numeric symbols, you will come up with valid filenames. Unlike the variables in an Icon program, they may begin with a numeric symbol. The Icon system takes this file and converts it into a machine-readable form. It takes the file name, chops off the period and "extension" as it is called; the three letters *icn* and this truncated form of the name become the name of the machine-readable file. In some implementations of Icon, the machine readable file ends in the extension *icx*. The original file (called the source file) continues to exist of course, and may be subsequently modified and reprocessed if necessary. The earlier machine-readable file will be deleted automatically by doing so.

Let us say that we have created a file called *average.icn* which contains an Icon program. We type in

> *icont average*

which submits the file *average.icn* to the Icon translator. Some intermediate files are created by the Icon system, but since they are later deleted, the programmer need not normally know anything about them. We may then make this translated file operate by typing in

> *iconx average*

whereby Icon executes the translated file which it has created. On some systems you can omit the *iconx* and simply type in the name of the machine-readable file (*average* in this case) which will then be executed. You can try that first, and if it does not work, you will have to use *iconx*. Icon files normally do not stand alone; the Icon system must be present when they are executing. The program may be run again at any time by repeating the last command. We may also write the two processes on one line thus:

> *icont average.icn -x*

where the *-x* argument tells the system to execute the file as soon as it has been processed. We shall learn how to handle data placed on a file in the next chapter.

4
Graphs

4.1 HISTOGRAMS

Now that we can record both data and programs in a permanent form, let us see how we may construct a frequency distribution graph in the form of a histogram and get it onto the screen. We want to represent the *word lengths* (from 1 up) along the horizontal axis so that the first spot represents words of one letter, the second spot words of two letters and so on. The vertical axis represents the *number of words* of each type (from 0 up) starting from the bottom of the grid. Using "X" to fill a particular spot in the grid (since, for the moment anyway, we do not have access to the traditional rectangle) we get a figure that may look like this:

```
         X X
         X X
         X.X
         X XX
         X XX
         X XX
         XXXXX
         XXXXX
         XXXXX
        XXXXXXX
        XXXXXXXX
       XXXXXXXXX X
       XXXXXXXXXXX
       XXXXXXXXXXXX X
       XXXXXXXXXXXXXXX
```

There ought, of course, to be some indication of what the X's signify, but we can ignore that for the moment. When we draw such a figure by hand it is natural to start at the base at the 0,0 coordinates and move left-to-right and upwards. Although techniques (known as "cursor control") can mimic this, it is more natural for the computer to start printing out at the top and move down in its normal manner. Let us assume for the moment that there will be a maximum of thirty words in any column (up-to-down) and a maximum of ten letters per word in any row (left-to-right). Starting at the row representing thirty, we need to move along it ten times, inserting an X if there are thirty words for that particular column and a blank if there are not. This will then be repeated for row twenty-nine, inserting an X if there are twenty-nine *or more* words for that particular column, and a blank if there are not. We can express the movement down the columns by

```
every n := 30 to 1 by -1 do
```

Each time this statement is reached, **every** will call up the next value counting *down* by -1, so each time the value of n is reduced by 1. The expression 30 to 1 by -1 is an Icon specialty called a generator, which we met in the last chapter counting *up* from 1 to 10. It produces a *group* of values {30,29,28...3,2,1} and **every** effectuates a loop that keeps on going just so long as the generator continues to produce something (which in this case is assigned to n and can be used inside the loop). We can express the movement along the rows by

```
every p := 1 to 10 do
```

It is not necessary to express the "by +1" (although we may put it in if we wish) since this is assumed if no other value is mentioned. Such an assumed value is known as a *default*. The number of the iteration at any particular time is stored in the variable p, just as before. We now place the "row loop" inside the "column loop":

```
every n := 30 to 1 by -1 do
   every p := 1 to 10 do
```

In this way the p-loop will itself be performed thirty times. During each iteration of the p-loop the value of n will be constant, while that of p increases each time. This procedure is then repeated, with the value of n being reduced by 1. Now we have to extract the information contained in the list `letters`. At each point on the grid we want to put in an X if the p-th item in the list contains a number *equal to or greater than* n. This is a good example how variables enable the computer to be a *general* machine and is expressed by the command

```
if letters[p] >= n then writes("X") else writes(" ")
```

There are several things to notice. First, the function **writes()** writes its argument to the screen, but unlike **write()** does *not* then proceed to the next line. When we get to the end of each row we are going to have to use **write()**, with its argument omitted, not to write anything, but simply to proceed to the next line. Second, the blank must be written expressly and comes in the other leg of the if-statement, beginning with the word **else**. Finally we need to note the symbol >= which means "is greater than or equal to." We now have:

```
every n := 30 to 1 by -1 do {
  every p := 1 to 10 do
    if letters[p] >= n then writes("X") else writes(" ")
  write()}
```

The curly brackets are needed because the outer loop has within it two statements (the inner loop and the command to proceed to the next line when that loop finishes). Now **do** expects to be followed by only one command; if there are more than one, they are enclosed within curly brackets. Notice how the indentation indicates the structure. The second **every** statement is controlled by the first, and so is indented. The **if** statement is controlled by the second **every** statement, and so is indented further. The **write()** statement is controlled by the *first* **every** statement, and so has the same indentation as the second **every** statement. Indentation is optional, but very helpful when looking at programs subsequently. The complete procedure now looks like this:

```
procedure histogram()
every n := 30 to 1 by -1 do {
  every p := 1 to 10 do
    if letters[p] >= n then writes("X") else writes(" ")
  write()}
end
```

If we call this procedure from the main procedure, our program looks like this:

```
global letters

procedure main()
  while word_length(read())
  read()
  printout()
  read()
  histogram()
end
```

```
procedure word_length(line)
local length
initial letters := list(10,0)
  line ?  while length := (write(*tab(many(&ucase ++
    &lcase)))) do {
  tab(many(' .,;:!'))
  letters[length] +:= 1}
return
end

procedure printout()
local n
  every n:= 1 to 10 do
    write("There are ",letters[n]," ",n,"-letter words.")
return
end

procedure histogram()
local n, p
  every n := 30 to 1 by -1 do {
    every p := 1 to 10 do
      if letters[p] >= n then writes("X") else writes(" ")
    write()}
return
end
```

Note that we specified n and p as *local variables* which function only in the procedure **histogram**, and we added **return** at the end of the procedure. The procedure would have worked quite well without these, since variables are assumed to function only within their procedure unless they are specified at the beginning as global, and **return** is similarly unnecessary, because the entire program concludes at this point anyway, but it is good practice to specify local variables, and to make the procedure return properly. Local variables are specified by placing the word **local** at the beginning of the procedure followed by the names of the variables separated by commas. Additionally we placed two **read()** commands in the main program. We did this because the output would appear on the screen and scroll off before it could be read, so this requires the user to press return in between the various sections of the program.

4.2   READING DATA FROM A FILE

We have already learned how to record the program in a permanent form and run it from the file in which it has been preserved. It is also possible, and often desirable, to record the data in a file. The program then reads the data from the file instead of reading from the keyboard. Using EDLIN, EMACS, or any other editor which uses the ASCII character set, create a file called *sample.txt* and type in a paragraph of text from a novel, poem, or any other source. We are distinguishing Icon source files by the "extension" *icn* and files containing texts by the extension *txt*. Instead of using the keyboard we wish to pull in the information from *sample.txt*, and we need some way of referring to this file in the program. The name itself will not do, since its value is simply a string of characters. Icon possesses a function **open()** which takes such a string as its argument, readies the file by that name for reading, and produces a value, which, unlike the string that names the file, *can* be used to reference it. This is then assigned to a variable of our choice:

```
infile := open("sample.txt")
```

We can now modify the preceding main procedure as follows:

```
procedure main()
local infile
  infile := open("sample.txt")
  while word_length(read(infile))
  close(infile)
  read()
  printout()
  read()
  histogram()
end
```

Material will now be read in, a line at a time, from the input file which is called "sample.txt" and is represented by the variable **infile**. When **read** attempts to produce material from the file after the last line has been read, **read** fails and the program moves on to the next item. When we have finished using the file we close it, using the function **close()**. In this instance there is no need to assign the value of **close()**, if any, to a variable since it would not be useful for any purpose. It is a good idea to close a file when it is not needed any more, since there may be limits on the number of files that can be open at one time. If this is omitted, however, Icon automatically closes all files when the program finishes.

The program as it stands at this point can only read from a file called *sample.txt*, which places a limit on the usefulness of the program. It is not general enough. It is worthwhile then to set up a separate procedure which will allow the user to determine what file is to be used. The *value* of this procedure will be the name of the file which the user wishes to use. Previously we have not used the values of procedures, but in this case it will be convenient to do so:

```
procedure getfilename()
local filename
  write("What is the name of the input file?")
  filename := read()
return filename
end
```

In this procedure we "prompted" the user to give the name of the file, and then returned it as the value of the procedure as a whole. In the preceding program, then, we replace the command

```
infile := open("sample.txt")
```

by

```
infile := open(getfilename())
```

After getfilename() returns the name of a file, we attempt to open it and assign it to infile. There is one further refinement which is desirable. What would happen if the user specified a file which does not exist? As it stands there would be eventually be a *run-time error*; that is to say, the Icon system would stop the program and issue a message stating that it attempted to read from a file that does not exist. These messages, however, are meant for you as a program developer, not for the end user. To avoid the user getting a message which might not be understood, instead of the command

```
infile := open(getfilename())
```

we can write

```
(infile := open(getfilename()) | stop("File does not exist!")
```

In this case Icon will try first to execute the command, now within parentheses on the left. The upright bar specifies an alternative ("or") in the event that that command cannot be fulfilled. The function stop() simply stops the program dead in its tracks and writes on the screen the message, if any, which is its argument. This enables us to stop the program gracefully in a manner of our own choosing if continuance is impossible, rather than having the Icon system throw up its hands in disgust and declare that the programmer did not allow for the user's carelessness.

There is an alternative possibility. We can set up a loop that will only function if the attempt to open a file is unsuccessful. It will then solicit a new attempt by the user. When eventually the user enters an appropriate filename, the loop ceases:

```
while not (infile := open(getfilename())) do
  write("File cannot be opened.  Please try again.")
```

In effect this means: "If the attempt to open the file is not successful, then
enter the loop; otherwise continue." After the logical expression **not** it is
a good idea to put what it controls in parentheses, otherwise it may attach
itself to part of what follows with unexpected results. If we wish, we may use
the word **until** instead of **while not**.[1] Our program has now expanded to
the following:

```
global letters

procedure main()
local infile
  while not (infile := open(getfilename())) do
    write("File cannot be opened.  Please try again.")
  while word_length(read(infile))
  read()
  printout()
  read()
  histogram()
end


procedure word_length(line)
local length
initial letters := list(10,0)
  line ?  while length := (write(*tab(many(&ucase ++
    &lcase)))) do {
  tab(many(' .,;:!'))
  letters[length] +:= 1}
return
end


procedure printout()
local n
  every n:= 1 to 10 do
    write("There are ",letters[n]," ",n,"-letter words.")
return
end
```

---

[1] Readers familiar with Pascal should be aware that in Icon these expressions are identical, and both check the control statement *before* the loop is entered.

```
procedure histogram()
local n, p
  every n := 30 to 1 by -1 do {
    every p := 1 to 10 do
      if letters[p] >= n then writes("X") else writes(" ")
    write()}
return
end

procedure getfilename()
local filename
  write("What is the name of the input file?")
  filename := read()
return filename
end
```

4.3   REFINING THE HISTOGRAM

If you try the preceding program you will see that the histogram is very crude.
It is squeezed into the left-hand side of the screen. If a text is chosen that
has more than twenty or so examples of a word of a particular length, the top
of the histogram will run off the screen. And the X's are not very attractive.
Let us try to remedy these failings in turn. Icon possesses a function right()
which produces the string which is its first argument padded out by blanks
on the left so that it fills up a string the length of its second argument. Thus
write("hi") will produce

hi

on the screen. write(right("hi",10)) will produce

        hi

on the screen, that is "hi" preceded by eight blanks to make up a total of ten.
Accordingly, right before the p-loop in histogram() we can add

```
writes(right(" ",10))
```

which will place ten blanks at the beginning of each line. If we would like to
start the line with the value at the point of the vertical axis we could use the
corresponding function writes(left(n,2)) which will write the value of n
left-justified in two spaces. Thus whether the numeral printed out has one or
two digits, the columns of the histogram will be in proper order. The second
problem can be solved by scaling. If we take the statement

```
every n := 30 to 1 by -1 do {
```

and change the steps, the value of a particular X is augmented. Thus 85 to 5 by -5 would allow for a total of 85 occurrences of words of a particular length, and each X would be equivalent to five occurrences. This will occupy only 18 lines on the screen and will of course treat occurrences of less than five as a non-event. These numbers can be adjusted in any way convenient.

Finding something to replace the X is a little more complicated because it involves using characters which cannot be input from the keyboard, and is dependent on the particular kind of screen you are using. All the characters of the ASCII character set have a number. Icon has a function `char()` which takes a number as its argument and returns the corresponding character as its value. So the value of `char(65)` is the uppercase A. As an exercise let us try to write a procedure to mimic what `char()` does. Let us call it `chr()`. Now Icon has several standard sets of characters. Such useful standard values are called "keywords" and are preceded by the character `&`. Thus `&ucase` is the set of all the capital letters from "A" to "Z". `&lcase` is the set of all the small letters from "a" to "z". `&digits` is the set of numbers from "0" to "9". `&ascii` is the set of the first 128 ASCII characters from 0 to 127. `&cset` is the set of all the ASCII characters from 0 to 255. This latter is known as the extended ASCII set. The characters from 128 to 255 may or may not have a graphic representation, according to the local conditions under which you are working. All we need to do is to find the correct character in the set and return it as the value of the function. This is achieved by the following:

```
procedure chr(n)
   if integer(n) then
      &cset ?  {move(n)
         return move(1)}
end
```

`&cset` is actually a set, in which the *order* of the components is not significant, but Icon converts this set to a string for this purpose. These automatic conversions are characteristic of Icon. They contribute to Icon's status as a "high-level" programming language and certainly save time for the programmer. `move()` moves that imaginary pointer as many slots as have been put into the procedure. Since the first character is number 0, the value of `move(n)` is a string from the beginning of the set right up to the character we wish to capture. Since this string is of no particular interest to us, no use is made of it and it is discarded. But the pointer has been moved up, and by moving it up one more and returning that one-character string as the value of the function, our goal has been achieved. Note carefully the difference between `move()` and `tab()`. The first moves up the pointer by adding the number of its argument to the current position of the pointer in the string. The second moves it to the position in the string stated in its argument. So if you are starting at the beginning of a string, `move(2)` brings you to

position 3 (since the first position is numbered 1), whereas `tab(2)` brings you
to position 2. Try running the following:

```
procedure main()
  printout()
end

procedure printout()
local n
  every n := 0 to 255 do {
#If program does not work properly remove next pound sign
  #if n ~= 26 then
    writes(right(n,3),"=",char(n)," ")
  if n % 13 = 0 then write()}
end
```

Now, if you like, you can change `char` to `chr`, include the `chr()` function
in the program and satisfy yourself that it works in exactly the same way.

Using the `right()` function in `printout()` ensures that most of the characters are lined up appropriately. The result is not completely satisfactory
because when some characters are written to the screen they cause special
movements of the cursor, such as number 8 which causes a backspace. The
percent sign represents the arithmetic modulo, i.e., it gives the remainder of
`n` divided by thirteen. This ensures that a maximum of thirteen items are
included on each line, each item including the ASCII number, an equal sign,
the corresponding character, and a space. For clearer examination of the
characters 128 and over, change

```
every n := 0 to 255 do {
```

to

```
every n := 128 to 255 do {
```

and

```
if n % 13 = 0 then write()}
```

to

```
if n % 13 = 0 then {write(); write()}}
```

The semicolon causes the following command to be considered as if it were a
separate command written on another line. The extra pair of curly brackets
is necessary so that both occurrences of `write()` are part of the **then** clause.
Try leaving them out, and figure out why the effect on the screen is what it
is. Also, try changing

```
n % 13 = 0
```

to

```
n % 13 = 10
```

and figure out why it produces a better-looking result on the screen.

Returning to our original problem, if we are lucky, we now have a choice of graphic-type characters that we might use to replace the X. 171, 177, 178, 219 may be possible candidates. Substitute char(171) (or another number) for the "X". In implementations that do not use the ASCII characters 128 to 255 for any graphic representation on the screen, you may try characters 24 and 26 which sometimes are represented by a rectangle on the screen.

SUMMARY OF ICON FEATURES

1. The expression **by -1** may be used in Icon to count down a loop.

2. A group of commands included inside curly brackets is treated as though the whole was a single command.

3. **return** is followed by the value of the function, if any, and indicates that the function has succeeded.

4. **open( )**

   value a *file variable* which may be used in a program to reference a file.

   effect prepares a file for use in a program.

5. **close( )**

   value its value is not useful, since the file it references is closed.

   effect closes a file, and prevents it from being further used in the program.

6. The upright bar (|) is the logical "or". If the expression preceding it fails, the one following it is tried.

7. **stop( )**

   effect concludes the program as soon as the message, if any, in its argument has been printed on the screen.

8. **right( )** and **left( )** control positioning on the screen by padding out the string which is the first argument by the number of blanks stated in the second argument. An optional third argument may use some other string instead of a blank.

9. Keywords are preceded by an ampersand sign and contain useful values. **&ucase** and **&lcase** are the upper- and lowercase set. **&ascii** is the set of the first 128 ASCII characters. **&cset** is the set of all 256 characters.

10. The percent sign produces the remainder of the numeral before it divided by the numeral after it.

11. **move()**

    value the string between the old and new positions of the pointer.

    effect moves up the pointer in a string being scanned the number of places stated in its argument.

5

Measures of Central Tendency

5.1 THE MODE

The mode represents the most common value, even though values almost as common may be very different from it. Our task is to take a text, divide it into three sections, and find the most common word-length in each. The task can be divided up as follows, and these subtasks will correspond to procedures in the program:

1. Get the name of the file containing the data and make sure that it actually exists.

2. Count the number of words in the file and divide by three.

3. Find out how many words of length 1 to 20 there are in the first third, find the most common value (the mode), and print out the results on the screen neatly; repeat this operation for the remaining two-thirds.

At this point it may prove convenient to devise a procedure which pulls a single word from a file every time it is called until the end of the file is reached. This procedure becomes in effect a "black box" as it is called; at one end an entire file enters, at the other the words pour out in sequence. Once we have the procedure, we can forget about how it works, and this is what the black box is: a *machine* which works without requiring the owner to know how. We just have to be sure to give it the right input and use the output appropriately. Our procedure operates much as a food processor turns vegetables into soup, although turning soup into vegetables might be

a closer analogy. We first need to define the characters which may occur in
words and the punctation marks (including the space) which mark them off.
This may be achieved tentatively by:

```
chars := (&lcase ++ &ucase ++ '1234567890\'-')
punct := ' .,?";:!'
```

The double plus signs are used for adding sets; we add the set of the
lowercase characters to the set of the uppercase characters and add to that
the numerals, the dash, and the apostrophe. Note that the apostrophe (or
"single quote") is preceded by a backslash. If we did not put it in, Icon
would assume we meant it as the closing marker of the set which is marked
off by single quote marks. There is a slight problem here: Does the word
"boy's", for example, contain four letters or five? This is really a matter
of definition, involving perhaps a distinction between letters and characters,
and for our purposes it will be simpler to assume five in this case. We can
cope with this problem later if necessary. Another problem will occur if single
quote marks are used in the file much as double quote marks are used. This
problem too can be coped with if necessary, but for the moment we may want
to be sure that our data uses single quote marks only as apostrophes. We
let the procedure know the name of the relevant file by including a variable
in the parameters of the procedure, i.e., in the parentheses which follow the
procedure name. The procedure heading will then be:

```
procedure getword(filename)
```

This file is opened by:

```
filvar := open(filename)
```

The function **open()** takes the filename, prepares the file for reading and
assigns a *file value* to the variable **filvar**. Note the difference between the
value of **filename** and **filvar**. The first is a string of characters which is the
name of the file. The second is the file itself. We assume that a check has
already been made that a file of this name actually exists, and will discuss
this later. We are now free to read a line from the file and chop it up into
words much as we did before. Instead of using **return** to precede the value
that will be the value of the procedure, we use **suspend**. This returns a value
just like **return**, but leaves everything in the procedure in place so that it can
continue when called again in an **every** loop. Normally, when a procedure
returns, all the variables it has employed disappear, thus making room in the
memory for storing other necessary information. But in this case a loop like

```
every write(getword(filename))
```

will produce every word in the file and write it to the screen. Here now is our
complete procedure:

```
procedure getword(filename)
#This procedure produces one word at a time from the file
local chars, punct, filvar, line, word
  chars := (&lcase ++ &ucase ++ '1234567890\'-')
  punct := ' .,?";:!'
  filvar := open(filename)
  while line := read(filvar) do
    line ?  {tab(many(' ')) #skip leading blanks
      while word := tab(many(chars)) do {
        tab(many(punct))
        suspend word}}
  close(filvar)
end
```

This procedure should always be used to process the entire file. If it is stopped at some point in the middle, and later resumed, the results may be unexpected.

For the first time we have added a *comment*. When Icon sees the pound sign # (also known as the number sign or crosshatch) it ignores it and the rest of the line. This enables us to make comments to aid the understanding of the program. These comments are written in normal English and can be as long as desired, provided each line or part of line begins with #. Another comment explains that we move up the imaginary pointer until just after any blanks that begin a line. This refers to indentation of course. When the file has been completely read, an attempt to read again fails, and the file is closed.

The preceding procedure makes it an easy matter to count the number of words in a file:

```
procedure countfile(filename)
#Counts the number of words in a file
local total
  total := 0
  every getword(filename) do
    total +:= 1
return total
end
```

Here we pass the name of the file (previously checked) to this procedure which simply calls **getword()** and counts the number of times that it works. This is done by setting the value of a local variable (called here **total**) to zero and incrementing it on each turn of the loop. The value of total becomes the value of the procedure. This can be captured by assigning it to a variable, or using it as the argument for some other function.

We mentioned that we have to have some way of getting a filename from the user and checking that the file actually exists. We suggested two ways of doing this: checking and stopping the program if the file does not exist, or alternatively keep on asking the user for a filename until a valid filename is received. It is possible to combine these two approaches. We can give the user a fixed number of tries, and then if it still isn't right, halt the program:

```
procedure get_valid_filename()
#This procedure gives user three chances to select a file
local filename
  every 1 to 3 do {
    writes("What is the name of the input file?  ")
    filename := read()
    if close(open(filename)) then return filename else
      write("Unable to open file.")}
  stop("Bye!")
end
```

Let us first look inside the **every** loop. The program solicits a filename which will be typed on the same line as the question since **writes** was used, and does not issue a carriage return. (There is a blank at the end of the question to make a small division.) Whatever is read in from the keyboard is stored in the variable **filename**. The command

```
close(open(filename))
```

attempts to open the file and immediately close it. The value produced by open() is simply fed immediately to close(). If the attempt is successful, then the string of characters which constitutes the name of the file is immediately returned as the value of the procedure, jumping clean out of the loop and the procedure. If this is *not* the case, a message is given to the user and the process is repeated. This can only be repeated a total of three times. If the third attempt fails, the loop is left normally, and the program is stopped with a farewell. You might ask why the file is not left open, since presumably we plan to use it. It is probably best to allow the procedures that need it to open their own files and close them when finished. Closing the file enables the next procedure which needs the file to start at the beginning. If a file is left open after use, we remain at the point reached in the file, which will generally be the "end of file" or *EOF*, as it is known. In this case there would be no problem, since the file has not been read, but it is best to get accustomed to closing files as soon as they are no longer needed.

Now we have to consider a procedure to do the actual work of processing the information we wish to display. getmodes(filename) receives the name of a valid filename from the main program, and will read as follows:

```
procedure getmodes(filename)
#Does the main work of the program
local filelength, limit, section, counter, letters, word
  filelength := countfile(filename)
  limit := (filelength / 3)
#Section is the numeric name of one of the sections
#of the file
  section := 0
#Counter triggers a printout when it reaches limit
  counter := 0
  letters := list(20,0)
  every word := getword(filename) do {
#Increment the appropriate element in the
#list of word-lengths
    letters[*word] +:= 1
    counter +:= 1
    if counter = limit then {
#Increment the section number, pass it to
#printout() with the list
      printout(section +:= 1,letters)
#Reinitialize letters and counter
      letters := list(20,0)
      counter := 0}}
return
end
```

The procedure contains a rather large number of local variables. The variable filelength holds the number of words in the file, and is found by using the procedure countfile. This number is divided into three and the result stored in the variable limit which is the number of words in each of the three sections we shall consider. The expression

```
limit := (filelength / 3)
```

contains an example of integer division. If one whole number is divided into another whole number, the result will be a whole number with any remainder discarded. Note that the number is not rounded to the nearest number. If we wanted the result expressed with a decimal, we should have to use 3.0 rather than 3, but this is not necessary here where we have no need to handle fractions of words. In this instance the variable filelength is not used much and we could save a variable by replacing the two commands

```
filelength := countfile(filename)
limit := (filelength / 3)
```

by

```
limit := (countfile(filename) / 3)
```

The variable `section` will be used to number the sections when we print them out. We shall make its initial value 0, then right before each time we use it, we shall increase its value by one. Similarly, the variable `counter` is initially zero, and will have its value increased by one each time we pull a word. When it reaches the limit, which is one-third of the file, it will trigger a printout of results so far, enabling the process to start over. The variable `letters` is a list of twenty variables, which will be used to hold the number of occurrences of a particular word length. Thus if there are five occurrences of four-letter words, the value of `letters[4]` will be 5; if there are ten occurrences of two-letter words, the value of `letters[2]` will be 10. The initial value of each member of the list is 0, and there are twenty members because we suppose that is the maximum likely length of any word in English. (The number would have to be higher for German, for example.) The variable `word` holds the current word that we are dealing with. Now let us see how the procedure works. A word is extracted from the file by `getword()`. Its length is ascertained by prefixing an asterisk and this is used as the index of the list

```
letters[*word]
```

which is increased by one. Each time we do this we check if the number of times it has been done is equal to the limit of one-third of the length of the file. When this occurs, we take time out to print what we have achieved so far by calling `printout()`, and when that has been done, return to `getmodes()`, reset the counter and all the elements of the list to 0 and start over with the next section of the text.

Now let us see what this diversion to `printout()` achieves. This procedure receives two pieces of information: the number of the section (from one to three) on which it is currently working, and the list containing the information which `getmodes()` has acquired. There are three local variables:

- `greatest`—holds the greatest value in the list.

- `n`—holds the current index from 1 to 20.

- `mode`—holds the index which points to the greatest value at any particular time, ultimately pointing to the greatest value of the entire list.

We simply print out the values in the list from the top down, and compare `greatest` which is initially zero with the particular value. If the value is greater, it replaces the current value of `greatest` and that particular index becomes the mode, and is stored in the variable `mode`. At the end we print that out too, and go back to `getmodes()`. Our complete program is now as follows:

```
#This program divides a text into three parts, finds the
#number of words of length 1-20, prints out a list of
#each and gives the mode in each case.
procedure main()
  getmodes(get_valid_filename())
end



procedure get_valid_filename()
#This procedure gives user three chances to open a file
local filename
  every 1 to 3 do {
    writes("What is the name of the input file?  ")
    filename := read()
    if close(open(filename)) then return filename else
      write("Unable to open file.")}
stop("Bye!")
end



procedure getword(filename)
#This procedure produces one word at a time from the file
local chars, punct, filvar, line, word
  chars := (&lcase ++ &ucase ++ '1234567890\'-')
  punct := ' .,?";:!'
  filvar := open(filename)
  while line := read(filvar) do
    line ?  {tab(many(' ')) #skip leading blanks
      while word := tab(many(chars)) do {
        tab(many(punct))
        suspend word}}
close(filvar)
end



procedure countfile(filename)
#Counts the number of words in a file
local total
  total := 0
  every getword(filename) do
    total +:= 1
return total
end
```

```
procedure getmodes(filename)
#Does the main work of the program
local filelength, limit, section, counter, letters, word
  filelength := countfile(filename)
  limit := (filelength / 3)
#Section is the numeric name of one of the sections
#of the file
  section := 0
#Counter triggers a printout when it reaches limit
  counter := 0
  letters := list(20,0)
  every word := getword(filename) do {
#Increment the appropriate element in the
#list of word-lengths
    letters[*word] +:= 1
    counter +:= 1
    if counter = limit then {
#Increment the section number,
#pass it to printout() with the list
      printout(section +:= 1,letters)
#Reinitialize letters and counter
      letters := list(20,0)
      counter := 0}
#end of the every loop
  }
return
end

procedure printout(p, l)
#prints out the info.  p is the section no., l is the list.
local greatest, n, mode
#Assume the lowest possible value for the most occurrences
#& correct it
  greatest := 0
  write("Section no.   ",p,".")
  write("Length      Number Such")
  every n := 20 to 1 by -1 do {
```

```
#Arrange info in columns
    write(right(n,2),right(l[n],12))
#Update greatest and mode if necessary
    if l[n] > greatest then {
      greatest := l[n]
      mode := n}
  } #end of the every loop
  writes(" ","Mode = ",mode)
  write(right("Press return to continue.", 52))
  read()
return
end
```

5.2   THE ARITHMETIC MEAN

The substitution of the arithmetic mean or average for the mode is quite
simple. The procedure printout() needs to know the number of words with
which it is dealing so that it can figure the mean. We achieve this by making
limit a global variable, which means that it can be used by all procedures in
the program. So we declare this variable at the very beginning of the program
preceded by the word global. We remove it as a local variable in getmodes()
which perhaps now we should call getmeans(). It would be possible to pass
this value to printout(), but since it never changes there is not much point,
and it might as well be stored once for all in limit. The beginning of our
program will now read as follows:

```
#This program divides a text into three parts, finds the
#number of words of length 1-20, prints out a list of
#each and gives the mean in each case.


global limit

procedure main()
  getmeans(get_valid_filename())
end
```

We set up a local variable in printout(), letter_total, to hold the total
number of letters. letter_total is initialized to 0, and at each turn of the
loop we increase it by the value of l[n] multiplied by n (i.e., the number of
words multiplied by the number of letters in those words). So our revised
printout() will look like this:

```
procedure printout(p, 1)
#prints out the info.  p is the section no., 1 is the list.
local letter_total, n
  letter_total := 0
  write("Section no.   ",p,".")
  write("Length        Number Such")
  every n := 20 to 1 by -1 do {
#Arrange info in columns and figure letter total
    write(right(n,2),right(1[n],12))
    letter_total +:= (n * 1[n])}
#Write out the mean
  writes(" ","Mean = ", real(letter_total) / limit)
  write(right("Press return to continue.", 52))
  read()
return
end
```

Note that we convert one of the items in the division to a real number (i.e., one with a decimal point) so that the result will be precise. If arithmetic functions are performed on numbers of which at least one is real, the answer will be real. The function **real()** converts an integer, or a string if feasible, into a real number. One question arises. What would happen if the file were empty? It might appear that we should divide by zero and thereby cause a run-time error. In point of fact there is no problem, because **getword()** will fail as soon as it is called, with the result that **printout()** will not be called at all. However, this is something to watch for. It is always a good idea to test a program by offering it unusual data, such as an empty file.

5.3 THE MEDIAN

In order to figure the median, only **printout()** needs to be changed from the form it took in the previous version of our program, although we may wish to change the name **getmeans()** to **getmedians()**. First we must get a list of cumulative frequencies, based on the list of frequencies which was prepared in **getmedians()**. We set up this totally distinct list in the same way as before:

```
lcf := list(20,0)
```

We now have a list called **lcf** containing twenty elements initialized to zero. The first value in the list is identical with the first value in the other list:

```
lcf[1]  := 1[1]
```

We then increment each value of the cumulative list by the next value in the other list, and that becomes the next value of the cumulative list:

```
every n := 2 to 20 do
   lcf[n] := (lcf[n - 1] + l[n])
```

Our list of cumulative frequencies is now complete. The parentheses are put in to ensure that the addition is done before any assignment is made to lcf[n]. Items within parentheses are always computed first, and their use may avoid an incorrect computation. It is often safer to put in parentheses than try to remember the priorities that Icon assigns, even though it is quite consistent in the manner in which this is done. We now compute the value which contains the median. We set an index n to zero and increase it so long as the corresponding value in the list of cumulative frequencies is less than half of the total:

```
#calculate vcm
   n := 0
   while lcf[n +:= 1] < (limit / 2.0)
   vcm := n
```

As soon as lcf[n] overshoots one-half of the total, the loop stops. This while loop contains only the expression which controls the loop, so the word do which normally introduces the body of the loop is missing altogether. This is in order, since we are interested in the value of n which is part of the controlling expression and increases until it becomes the number we are seeking. It is then the number of the value containing the median and is stored in vcm. We can now compute the median by subtracting 0.5 from the value containing the median (since the upper range of the next value down is in between the two values) and add it to the cumulative frequency of the lower value subtracted from one-half of the total divided by the frequency of the value containing the median. This gives us the following:

```
#calculate median
   median := ((vcm - 0.5) +
      ((limit / 2.0 - lcf[vcm - 1]) / l[vcm]))
```

with the entire procedure as follows:

```
procedure printout(p, l)
local lcf, vcm, n #lcf is a list of cumulative frequencies,
#vcm is the value which contains the median, n is the index
#The procedure prints out the info.  p is the section no., l
#is the list of frequencies.
```

```
#calculate lcf
lcf := list(20,0)
lcf[1] := l[1]
every n := 2 to 20 do
  lcf[n] := (lcf[n - 1] + l[n])
#calculate vcm
  n := 0
  while lcf[n +:= 1] < (limit / 2.0)
  vcm := n
#calculate median
  median := ((vcm - 0.5) +
    ((limit / 2.0 - lcf[vcm - 1]) / l[vcm]))
#Arrange info in columns
  write("Length      Number Such")
  every n := 20 to 1 by -1 do
    write(right(n,2),right(l[n],12))
  writes(" ","Median = ", median)
  write(right("Press return to continue.", 52))
  read()
return
end
```

5.4 VARIANTS ON THE PROGRAM

You may wish to try modifying these programs to do slightly different tasks.
For example, you could remove the feature of splitting the text into three
and allow it to find the various averages for an entire text. You could solicit
the user to tell you into how many pieces the text should be split before
proceding. This would need a prompt for the user, and the response would
be stored in a variable which would replace the fixed number three. Note
that in this case it would be a good idea to check that the user enters a valid
number. One way to do this is to use the function **integer( )** which converts
its argument to an integer if that is possible, and fails if it is not. Hence, if the
user would enter q instead of 2 the function would fail and an error message
could be issued. You might get one program to print out on the screen several
averages. You might include more than one version of printout, giving them
different names to keep them distinct, and call each version. It would be a
good idea to make a copy of a working program with a different name and
use the copy for experimentation of this type.

SUMMARY OF ICON FEATURES

1. The union of sets may be achieved by using the double plus sign (++). The double minus (--) and double multiplication sign (**) may similarly be used for set difference and intersection.

2. If we wish to include a single quote in a set (itself delineated by single quotes) we must precede the single quote with a backslash(\).

3. The word **suspend** returns a value from a procedure, but leaves the current status of the procedure in place for another call.

4. Comments may be inserted freely in a program provided that on each line they are preceded by the number sign (#).

5. If one integer (whole number) is divided by another integer, any remainder is discarded. A calculation which contains a real number (one with a decimal point) will result in a real number.

6. Global variables, which are available to all procedures in the program, must be declared at the beginning of the program preceded by the word **global**.

7. The function **real()** converts its argument to a real number (one with a decimal point) if it is possible, and fails otherwise.

8. Normally multiplication and division have precedence over addition and subtraction, but this order may be changed by using parentheses. Operations within parentheses are always done first. Thus $2 + 5 * 8$ evaluates to 42, while $(2 + 5) * 8$ evaluates to 56. It is a good idea to use parentheses freely, in nonarithmetic expressions also, for clarity and to avoid unexpected results.

6
Foreign Language Fonts

6.1 THE EXTENDED ASCII CHARACTER SET

Computers have grown up in a largely English-speaking world and hence the characters they use are mostly English characters. The possibilities of using foreign characters vary a good deal from one computer to another but we shall consider in this chapter the possibility of using foreign character sets on the IBM PC or compatible machines, since many readers will be using Icon on these machines and may wish to use a foreign character set. Let us consider first getting foreign characters up on the screen. Computers use various sets of characters, and some further detail of how these developed is given in Appendix A. The available characters are numbered, and those numbered from 128 to 255 contain characters useful for foreign languages, as well as mathematical symbols and designs that can be used for borders or emphasis. One way of entering these characters is to hold down the Alt key, then type in the character number on the keypad and release the Alt key. But this is rather cumbersome. Let us first write a program that will enable us to look at these characters and perhaps decide which we wish to use. We shall write a procedure called **showchars()** as follows. We start with **write()** just in order to move down the screen a little. In effect we wrote nothing and issued a carriage return. Icon has a function called **center()** which takes the string which is its first argument and centers it inside blanks, the total length of the string being specified in the second argument. (We can optionally add a third argument—if we do not want blanks for the padding, what we do want is placed there). So

```
write(center("THE EXTENDED ASCII CHARACTER SET",80))
```

will center the quoted phrase on the eighty-character line on the screen. We now put in another

```
write()
```

for appearance' sake. Now we can use the function **char()** referred to in
Chapter 4 to produce each character, and by placing it in a loop we can
produce the entire set:

```
every n := 128 to 255 do
  writes(char(n))
```

Remember that **every** keeps on going so long as the expression following it
produces something—and the expression **128 to 255** produces each of the
integers from 128 to 255 and assigns it each time to the variable n.

We can improve this simple loop by identifying each character:

```
every n:= 128 to 255 do
  writes(n," = ",char(n),"    ")
```

This will print on the screen over and over the current value of n; a blank, an
equals sign, and a blank; the ASCII character corresponding to n; and three
blanks. This creates a string of eight characters, and since this divides evenly
into 80, which is the number of characters that can appear on a line of the
screen, the output will appear in neat columns. This is an appropriate place
to consider how to handle matters if the number does not divide so neatly.
Let us try the command

```
writes(n," = ",char(n)," ")
```

This time we have only one blank at the end, with the result that the string
of characters is six in each case. A little arithmetic will show that we can get
thirteen such strings onto a line ($13 \times 6 = 78$), but then we must proceed to
the next line, otherwise the output will be uneven—unesthetic even though
legible. This can be done by using an Icon function *modulo* or *remainder*
which is expressed by placing the percent sign in between two integers. This
gives the *remainder* when the first is divided by the second. Thus, the value
of 13 % 3 is 1, and so is the value of 16 % 3. Accordingly we can each time
check the value of n, and if division by 13 leaves a remainder of 10, we issue a
carriage return. The remainder 10 is chosen because we start with the value
of 128, which leaves a remainder of 11 when divided by 13, and the number
will only get back to 10 after thirteen strings have been printed out. Note
that in the previous case we did not need a carriage return, since the full
eighty characters had been used and so the output went to the next line in
any case. Our revised procedure now looks as follows:

```
every n:= 128 to 255 do {
  writes(n," = ",char(n)," ")
  if n % 13 = 10 then write()}
```

Note that we now need the curly brackets because there is more than one command in the loop. Since we have packed more into one line we could now put a blank line between lines, without running off the screen:

```
every n:= 128 to 255 do {
writes(n," = ",char(n)," ")
if n % 13 = 10 then {write(); write()}}
```

The then-leg of the condition now requires curly brackets because it contains more than one statement. It is possible to place more than one statement on a line by using the semicolon, so here we have used the semicolon to mark off a new statement which we would usually put on another line. We must close both sets of curly brackets appropriately. This use of the remainder is often helpful in formatting for the screen. For example you might use it to figure when to issue a read() at the end of a screenful of text, in order to give the user a chance to indicate that more is wanted by pressing return.

Here is our complete program:

```
procedure main()
  showchars()
end

procedure showchars()
local n
  write()
  write(center("THE EXTENDED ASCII CHARACTER SET",80))
  write()
  every n := 128 to 255 do {
    writes(n,"=",char(n)," ")
    if n % 13 = 10 then {write(); write()}}
end
```

6.2 A CHARACTER SET FOR GERMAN

Let us suppose that we want to set up a character set on the screen for German. Of interest to us are six characters with an umlaut (Ä, Ö, Ü, ä, ö, ü), which are characters 142, 153, 154, 132, 148, 129, respectively, and a character to represent ß. For the latter we can use number 225 which is really a Greek beta, but quite close enough. One way we can handle this is to redefine the meanings of some keys (seven in this example) on the keyboard. To do this, go through the following steps.

  1. Ensure that you have the MS-DOS file ANSI.SYS on the disk with which you boot your computer. If it is on another disk, it should be

copied onto the disk you are using, and be sure that you have some room left over, perhaps by removing some files you do not need.

2. Create a file called CONFIG.SYS with EDLIN or some other editor and include in it the command

    DEVICE=ANSI.SYS

3. Save the following program in a file:

```
procedure main()
  setkeys()
end

procedure setkeys()
  writes("\e[0;59;129p")
  writes("\e[0;60;132p")
  writes("\e[0;61;142p")
  writes("\e[0;62;148p")
  writes("\e[0;63;153p")
  writes("\e[0;64;154p")
  writes("\e[0;65;225p")
end
```

4. Boot again, with ANSI.SYS in place.

5. Translate and run the program that you saved.

This program has the effect of changing the values of the function keys F1 to F7 so that they represent the special German characters. It works as follows. It purports to write seven strange-looking strings to the screen. In fact, the seven commands do nothing to the screen. \e is Icon's way of representing the *Escape* or *Esc* character that you see on your keyboard. This Escape character itself indicates that the symbols following are meant for some special purpose. So [0;62;148p means "Take the key represented by 0;62 (which is the F4 key) and make it represent the 148th character in the ASCII character set." The *p* is part of the instruction. There is nothing magic about the strange format of this instruction; the symbols are chosen arbitrarily by the designer of the system. In this string any number between 59 and 68 can occur after the first semicolon to represent the F-keys. The last number is any number in the ASCII character set. If it is used to change a key other than an F-key the *0;* at the beginning is omitted, and the ASCII number of that key inserted.

We said earlier that it is a good idea to keep data out of programs, and make them as general as possible. We might apply that idea here, and revise our program as follows:

```
procedure main(keylist)
  if 1 <= *keylist <= 10 then
    setkeys(keylist) else
    stop("Enter up to ten ASCII num_
      bers when running program.")
end

procedure setkeys(keylist)
local n, s
  s := 58
  n := 0
  while n < *keylist do
    if integer(keylist[n +:= 1]) then
      writes("\e[0;" || (s +:= 1) || ";" ||
        keylist[n] || "p")
end
```

The word *numbers* was broken to show that a string may be spread over more than one line by connecting with an underline. The underline will not appear on the screen. You will notice that this time the main procedure has a parameter. The value of this parameter is obtained from the line with which the user invokes the program. So if our program is in a file called *sample* then if

   iconx sample 123 124

is typed in, keylist will be a list of two strings; keylist[1] will have the value "123"; and keylist[2] will have the value "124". Note that the various elements on the call line are separated by blanks. If for some reason you want to include a blank in one of those elements, then the element containing the blank must be enclosed in double quotes which will be dropped when this element occurs in the list.[1] Our program first checks that our list is not less than one and not more than ten elements in length, since this program is going to make use of at least one and not more than ten F-keys. If this is not the case, the program is halted. Notice the format of the line which specifies the number of elements. This could also be expressed using the logical *and* which is represented in Icon by the ampersand:

```
if ((*keylist >= 1) & (*keylist <= 10)) then
  setkeys(keylist)
```

---

[1] For this reason it is best to avoid the necessity of including "real" double quotes in these items, although it can be done. If they occur within a string that is itself in double quotes because it contains blanks, then the real double quotes must be preceded by a backslash (\). Inside a single word the double quotes may have the backslash or omit it.

However, this requires looking up the length of **keylist** twice, and is more difficult to read. The prejudice against this kind of needless evaluation comes from the days when computer time was very expensive and there was a need to be frugal. But elegant programming demands brevity, and it is worth considering such issues in developing a programming style, much as it is in learning to write good English. You might want to try soliciting the information from the user, rather than looking for it on the command line; or perhaps offering both options: If there is something on the command line use it, if not, solicit it.

Let us look now at **procedure setkeys()**. The local variable n will be used for the index of **keylist[n]**. The local variable s is initialized to 58 which is one less than the number that refers to the first of the F-keys. The loop will run as many times as there are elements in **keylist**, which is measured by ***keylist**. The asterisk produces the length of a list just as it produces the length of a string of characters. We then build up, piece by piece, that string which gives the instruction to redefine the key. The incoming piece of information is first checked to make sure that it is an integer, and not, say, the letter a. While this check is being done, the variable n is increased by 1, so the very first time around it has the value 1. The variable s has the value 59, therefore (assuming the first number in the command line is 129) "\e[0;" 59 ";" "129" "p" are combined into

"\e[0;59;129p"

and this has the effect of making *ü* the value of the F1 key. Note that Icon automatically converts **59** from an integer to a string. We wanted this one to be an integer initially so that it might be increased in value automatically.

6.3 ANOTHER MODE OF SUBSTITUTION

Another way of handling our needs is to sacrifice some characters on our keyboard which will serve for the characters we need. For example, we might set up the following table:

ASCII number	Character to be replaced
129	{
132	}
142	~
148	'
153	|
154	&
225	@

Now we can use the Icon function `map()` which produces a string in which the first argument has each letter occurring in the second argument replaced with a corresponding letter in the third argument. Our procedure is as follows:

```
procedure umlaut(str)
static s
  initial s := (char(129) || char(132) || char(142) ||
    char(148) || char(153) || char(154) ||
    char(225))
return map(str,"{}~`|&@",s)
end
```

The variable **s** is declared as a static variable so that it will not have to be computed every time the procedure is called. An initial assignment of a string is made to **s** consisting of seven characters which are joined together by the symbol | | which is used to concatenate, or add together, strings of characters. These can all be on one line on the screen, although you will only be able to see the part of the line where the cursor happens to be located. It is important that the variables in an **initial** assignment should be global if they are to be used throughout the program, or static if they are to be used in one procedure only, because otherwise their value will be null when the procedure is called again. The function **map()** then takes the string which constitutes the first argument, and replaces each character there which occurs in the second argument with the corresponding character in the third.

How can we use this in practice? Well, we can create data files of German text in which instead of the German character ß we write **@**, instead of ö we write ', and so on. Then a program converts these files to files containing the special characters:

```
global infilename, outfilename

procedure main()
  get_valid_filenames()
  convert_file()
end

procedure get_valid_filenames()
  every n := 1 to 3 do {
    writes("What is the name of the input file?  ")
    infilename := read()
    if close(open(infilename)) then break else
      write("Unable to open file.")
    if n = 3 then stop("Bye.")}
```

```
    every n := 1 to 3 do {
      writes("What is the name of the output file?  ")
      outfilename := read()
      if close(open(outfilename)) then {
        write("File already exists.  Overwrite?  (y/n) ")
        if read() == "y" then break}
      else break}
  return
  end

  procedure convert_file()
  local infilvar, outfilvar
    infilvar := open(infilename)
    outfilvar := open(outfilename,"w")
    while line := read(infilvar) do
      write(outfilvar,umlaut(line))
    close(infilvar)
    close(outfilvar)
    write("File ",infilename," trans_
      ferred to ",outfilename)
  end

  procedure umlaut(str)
  static s
  initial s := (char(129) || char(132) || char(142) ||
    char(148) || char(153) || char(154) || char(225))
  return map(str,"{}~'|&@",s)
  end
```

Let us consider this program. First, we need two files: one which has the original data and one to receive the new data which has been derived from the old via our program. The file containing the original data *must* exist, because otherwise there will be nothing to read. The second need not exist: If it does, the user must be ready to have what is already there destroyed by the new data; if it does not exist, it will be created. We shall set up two global variables, accessible to all procedures, to hold the two filenames. The first loop is much like the procedure get_valid_filename() which we used previously. If the file is found to exist (which is established by successfully opening and closing it) then the expression **break** takes us out of the loop to continue to get the other filename. Otherwise we give two more tries to find a file, stopping the program if at the count of three we have not succeeded. There would then be no point in getting the second filename. If we successfully get the first filename, we go on to solicit the second. If it exists, we first check that the user is aware that it exists before going ahead.

This reduces the chance of the loss of valuable data by accident. We compare the response (the value of read()) with the string "y" (conventionally used for "yes"), and if it is equivalent, we proceed. (You might consider how to give the user a little more freedom. For example, with the help of upto() you might allow for "yes" or even "yeah" by looking for a y in the string, or allow for capitals by converting whatever comes in to small letters.) The symbol == is used for the comparison of strings. If it does not already exist, we shall be able to create it later using the function open() with a second argument "w" which enables new data to be written on the file. This is not needed when opening a file which only needs to be read.[2]

The procedure convert_file() simply reads the input file line by line, submits the line to umlaut() for modification, then writes it out to the output file.

SUMMARY OF ICON FEATURES

1. The value of center() is its first argument centered in blanks, the total length being the second argument. Blanks may be replaced by the character or characters occurring in the optional third argument.

2. Separate commands may be placed on one line if separated by semi-colons.

3. The *Escape* or *Esc* character is represented inside a string by \e. This character generally indicates that the rest of the string has a coded meaning for the computer such as key reassignment or moving the cursor to some designated point on the screen.

4. The double equal sign (==) may be used to compare strings.

5. A static variable retains its value between one call of a procedure and the next. Variables normally return to null value when the procedure finishes. This provides "memory" for the procedure.

6. The function open() may take an optional second argument "w" which allows the file to be written to. Data previously there will be destroyed unless the second argument is "a", in which case it will be appended to data there already. Note that these arguments must be enclosed in double quotes, or must be a variable valued at the characters w or a.

---

[2]The function open() automatically ensures that files are in UNIX format. You can inhibit this by adding the letter "u" (which stands for the strange word "untranslate") to the second argument. This technicality which you need not worry about is explained in Appendix A.

7
Standard Deviation

7.1 WORKING WITH SENTENCES

Our main task in this chapter is to find the standard deviation of the sentence length of a text, sentence length being measured by the number of words the sentence contains. Let us begin by developing a procedure to produce sentences from a file analogous to the one which produced words from a file. In this way we can build up a library of procedures which may have various applications. We shall find later that it is not necessary to spell out these procedures in every program. We can preprocess a group of them, and link them to our programs by adding a declaration at the beginning, but we need not know how to do that just now.[1] Let us first define a sentence as a string of characters ending in a period, a question mark, or an exclamation point. This definition is probably inadequate, because it may not be allowing for quoted sentences, but it will do for now. This does show us incidentally that programming often forces us to consider issues which we tend to overlook, since the computer requires us to be totally explicit. Let us observe first that the sentence can be longer or shorter than the line. The line is of a length that happens to be convenient for human beings to handle on the printed page or screen, and hence text files are traditionally divided into lines, which are about the length of a punched card—i.e., eighty characters—although the computer can handle lines of any length. When we bring in a line for handling, we must allow for the fact that the sentence which we wish to isolate can potentially be shorter or longer than the line. We are going first to bring in lines from the file as long as there are lines to bring, so we can safely start off with the now familiar loop

---

[1] Details may be found in Appendix D.

63

```
while line := read(filvar)
```

which brings in lines from a file until there are no more to bring, whereupon
it fails. We assume that we have already checked that **filvar** refers to the
relevant file. **markers** will hold the set of characters that can finish the
sentence and mark it off. The variable **line** will hold the current line of the
file with which we are dealing. The variable **sentence** will hold the string
of characters that will ultimately constitute a sentence by our definition, and
will be returned as one of the values of the procedure. The variable **substring**
will hold the string of characters from the beginning of the line up to a marker.
This could be a complete sentence, or it could be the end section of a sentence
that is several lines long. Now we set **sentence** to "", a valid string of zero
length, and go looking for one of the sentence markers. So often as we find
one, we have delineated a sentence, and can return it as one of the values
of the procedure. Accordingly we try to find a marker, and if we do, add
that section of the line, including the marker, to **sentence**, in case there is
something there already from a previous line. This activity is analogous to
incrementing a number. Recall that the statement

```
letters[n] +:= 1
```

adds 1 to **letters[n]** and stores the resulting number in **letters[n]**. So

```
sentence ||:= substring
```

adds **substring** to sentence, or, as we say, concatenates it, and then stores
the new augmented string in **sentence**. The double bar (||) is used for
the concatenation of strings. Of course, initially we shall just be adding the
section of the line to the zero-length string that **sentence** is at first. We
then return this value, reset **sentence** to the zero-length string, skip over
any blanks beginning the next sentence, and try again. If we fail and are at
the end of the line, we can just go fetch another line (if any are left) and
repeat the process. So we have so far:

```
sentence := ""
while line := read(filvar) do
  line ?  while substring := tab(upto(markers)) do {
    sentence ||:= (substring || tab(many(markers)))
    suspend sentence
    tab(many(' '))
    sentence := ""}
```

But what if we are not at the end of a line? This would imply that there
is something left in the line, or possibly the entire line which has not been
taken care of. We can test for this by the function **pos()**. This function

takes a single numeric argument and succeeds if its argument corresponds to the position of that imaginary pointer. 0 is the position right after the last character on the line, or perhaps more accurately, the initial position going from right to left. These positions start from 1 at the far left just before the first character and add one as you move right (1, 2, 3...), or from 0 at the far right just after the last character and subtract one as you move left (0, -1, -2...). It is possible then to indicate the position of the pointer positively from the left, beginning at 1, or negatively from the right, beginning at 0. Accordingly, **pos(0)** will succeed if the imaginary pointer is right at the end. If it is, we don't have to do anything. If it is not, we want to add what is left to the sentence, plus a space to allow for the fact that we don't normally put in a space at the end of the line:

```
if not pos(0) then
  sentence ||:= (line[&pos:0] || " ")}
```

&pos is a keyword which always contains the current position of the imaginary pointer, so

```
line[&pos:0]
```

represents the portion of **line** from the position of the pointer up to the end. This is added to **sentence**, a space is added, and we are ready to start over. Observe that like **do**, the **?** which marks the scanning facility expects one statement, so we must use the curly brackets if there are more than one. Here is the complete procedure:

```
procedure get_sentence(filename)
local filvar, sentence, line, substring, markers
  markers := '.!?'
  filvar := open(filename)
  sentence := ""
  while line := read(filvar) do
    line ?  {while substring := tab(upto(markers)) do {
      sentence ||:= (substring || tab(many(markers)))
      suspend sentence
      tab(many(' '))
      sentence := ""}
    if not pos(0) then
      sentence ||:= (line[&pos:0] || " ")}
close(filvar)
end
```

It is worthwhile working through this procedure one step at a time with various types of sentences to see how it works. Let us take, for example, a

file which begins with a sentence that takes up the whole of the first line
and concludes with a period in the middle of the second line. The value of
sentence is an empty string. line acquires the value of the first line of the
file. The while loop looks for a marker and fails, so the loop is never entered,
and the value of &pos remains at 1 as it was initially. Since it is *not* at the
end of the line, the if-statement right after the loop applies, and the value of
line[1:0]—which is in effect the entire line—is added to the string of zero
length, along with a blank, and stored in sentence. Notice the productive
way in which a zero-length string can be used; it enables us to treat the
initial build-up of the string in exactly the same way as the subsequent ones.
Initialization to zero in arithmetic computations gives analogous benefits.[2]
The next line is then fetched from the file. Again, an attempt is made at
the entry of the while-loop to find a marker, and this time it succeeds, so the
loop is entered. The characters up to the marker are stored in substring,
then this plus the following marker are added to sentence. The sentence is
now complete, and returned as the value of the procedure by suspend which
puts everything on hold until the process can continue. When it does, any
blanks following the sentence just processed are skipped, and &pos now has
the value of the position right after those blanks. sentence is reset to the
empty string so as to be ready for the next sentence. The loop is attempted
again, but fails. The if-statement is checked and succeeds, because &pos does
not indicate that the pointer is at the end. So the piece of the line from the
beginning of the new sentence until the end of the line plus a blank are stored
in sentence and we are ready to look for the rest of the line.

Let us consider a different possibility. Imagine our line consists of three
short sentences, so the last character on the line is a period. The while-loop
succeeds, and the first sentence is returned. The loop succeeds a second and
third time, each time returning a sentence. On the fourth try the loop fails.
Since the pointer is right at the end of the line the if-statement fails, and a
new line is brought in for processing.

We now need the ability to count the words in a sentence, and to do so
we modify and simplify two procedures we have used already:

```
procedure getword_from_sentence(sentence)
#This procedure produces one word at a time from the
#sentence
local chars, punct, word
  chars := (&lcase ++ &ucase ++ '1234567890\'-')
  punct := ' .,?";:!'
```

---

[2]Readers familiar with SNOBOL-4 will be aware that this represents a less easygoing
approach than SNOBOL-4, in which the initial value of a variable is the empty string,
which can function too as zero. This casualness may often save time and effort, but also it
can lead to subtle programming errors.

```
      sentence ?  {tab(many(' ')) #skip leading blanks
        while word := tab(many(chars)) do {
          tab(many(punct))
          suspend word}}
  end

  procedure countsentence(sentence)
  #Counts the number of words in a sentence
  local total
    total := 0
    every getword_from_sentence(sentence) do
      total +:= 1
  return total
  end
```

The procedure getword_from_sentence() is like getword(), but it does not have to concern itself with opening a file. The procedure countsentence() uses getword_from_sentence() to count the number of words in a sentence.

We are now ready for a procedure which will do the main work of the program. This will be simpler than our previous program in that it does not have to divide the text into parts, but it will also use a procedure to calculate the standard deviation as well as the mean.

7.2 FIGURING THE STANDARD DEVIATION

Let us consider the following procedure:

```
  procedure getav(filename)
  #Does the main work of the program
  local counter, words, sentence
    words := list(20,0)
    counter := 0
    every sentence := get_sentence(filename) do {
  #Increment the appropriate element in the list
  #of sentence-lengths
      words[countsentence(sentence)] +:= 1
      counter +:= 1}
    printout(words, counter)
  return
  end
```

Remember that the while-loop succeeds so long as the control statement at its head *succeeds*. The every-loop succeeds so long at the control statement at its head *produces a result*, and it prompts the statement to produce all the results in turn. Observe that a while-loop being controlled by a generator may go on perpetually, since only the first item that the generator may produce will be called up. This will be successful, but the next time around the same result will be produced, unless some effort is made within the loop to alter that situation. The variable **sentence** will hold the sentences in the file in succession. The number of words in the sentence is found by **countsentence(sentence)** and the corresponding element in the list **words** is increased by 1. We also have a counter which is increased in value each time the loop is entered and thus counts the total number of sentences in the file. When the job of **getav()** is done, it passes the information it has stored in the list **words** and the total number of sentences to **printout()**, which will figure the mean, call a procedure to figure the standard deviation, and print out the results. Let us look at these.

```
procedure printout(w,c)
#prints out the info. c is th  total # of
#sentences w is the list.
local word_total, n
  write("Length      Number Such")
  word_total := 0
  every n := 20 to 1 by -1 do {
#Arrange info in columns
    write(right(n,2),right(w[n],12))
    word_total +:= (n * w[n])}
  mean := real(word_total) / c
  writes(" ","Mean = ", mean)
  writes(right("Standard deviation = ", 42))
  write(standard_deviation(w,c,mean))
return
end

procedure standard_deviation(w,c,mean)
local sum_of_squares, n, st_dev
  sum_of_squares := 0
  every n := 1 to 20 do
    sum_of_squares +:= (((n - mean) ∧ 2) * w[n])
    st_dev := ((real(sum_of_squares) / c) ∧ 0.5)
return st_dev
end
```

printout() works in a similar way to the previous chapter, but it is only called once since it is processing the entire file. We already know the sentence total. We figure the word total by running through the list and multiplying the total words in a particular sentence by the number of times that that length sentence occurs. We pass on this information to `standard_deviation()` which is ready to do the calculation. Our local variables are n which serves as an index; `sum_of_squares` (which speaks for itself) and `st_dev` which will be the final value that we want. Initially `sum_of_squares` is set to zero and n is set to 1. The mean supplied by `printout()` is subtracted from 1 and this is squared. In Icon the symbol caret or wedge (∧) is used for exponentiation, and so n ∧ 2 achieves this end. On some keyboards or screens the circumflex (^) or the up-arrow (↑) may appear. All three represent the same character, ASCII 94. This is then multiplied by the number of times that that value is needed, which is stored in the first element of the list. It might be noted that if that number is zero the entire calculation is pointless because the ultimate result is zero. This could be taken care of by introducing a condition:

```
if w[n] ~= 0 then
   sum_of_squares +:= (((n - mean) \ 2) * w[n])
```

The Icon symbol ~= means "does not equal." (The symbol ~ is called a *tilde*.) This will inhibit the calculation if it is unnecessary. However, in this case the value of `w[n]` has to be fetched each time, causing additional computing if the value of `w[n]` is greater than zero, so it is probably not worthwhile to add this provision. Notice that there is still no need to insert a curly bracket after the do because the if-statement is a single statement, including its else-leg if it has one. Finally the standard deviation is figured by getting the mean and taking its square root (using a fractional exponent.)

Here is the complete program:

```
procedure main()
   getav(get_valid_filename())
end

procedure get_valid_filename()
local filename
#This procedure gives user three chances to
#select a file
   every 1 to 3 do {
     writes("What is the name of the input file?  ")
     filename := read()
     if close(open(filename)) then return filename else
        write("Unable to open file.")}
   stop("Bye!")
end

procedure getword_from_sentence(sentence)
#This procedure produces one word at a time from
#the sentence
```

```
local chars, punct, word
  chars := (&lcase ++ &ucase ++ '1234567890\'-')
  punct := ' .,?";:!'
  sentence ?  {tab(many(' ')) #skip leading blanks
    while word := tab(many(chars)) do {
      tab(many(punct))
        suspend word}}
end



procedure countsentence(sentence)
#Counts the number of words in a sentence
local total
  total := 0
  every getword_from_sentence(sentence) do
    total +:= 1
return total
end



procedure getav(filename)
#Does the main work of the program
local counter, words, sentence
  words := list(20,0)
  counter := 0
  every sentence := get_sentence(filename) do {
#Increment the appropriate element in the list
#of sentence-lengths
    words[countsentence(sentence)] +:= 1
    counter +:= 1}
  printout(words, counter)
return
end



procedure printout(w, c)
#prints out the info.  c is the total # of sentences
#w is the list.
local word_total, n, mean
  write("Length     Number Such")
  word_total := 0
  every n := 20 to 1 by -1 do {
```

```
#Arrange info in columns
    write(right(n,2),right(w[n],12))
    word_total +:= (n * w[n])}
  mean := real(word_total) / c
  writes(" ","Mean = ", mean)
  writes(right("Standard deviation = ", 42))
  write(standard_deviation(w,c,mean))
return
end

procedure get_sentence(filename)
local filvar, sentence, line, substring,markers
  markers := '.!?'
  filvar := open(filename)
  sentence := ""
  while line := read(filvar) do
#look for a marker
    line ?  {while substring := tab(upto(markers)) do {
#if one is found add it to sentence plus the marker
      sentence ||:= (substring || tab(many(markers)))
      suspend sentence
#skip blanks at beginning of next sentence
      tab(many(' '))
      sentence := ""}
#if the line is not finished, append the rest
#to sentence
    if not pos(0) then
      sentence ||:= (line[&pos:0] || " ")}
  close(filvar)
end

procedure standard_deviation(w,c,mean)
local sum_of_squares, n, st_dev
  sum_of_squares := 0
  every n := 1 to 20 do
    sum_of_squares +:= (((n - mean) ^ 2) * w[n])
  st_dev := ((real(sum_of_squares) / c) ^ 0.5)
return st_dev
end
```

7.3 WORD FREQUENCY

Using the preceding procedures we have designed, it is not difficult to construct a program which will check the frequencies of particular words. Our

main procedure will have a parameter word_list which means that when the program is run, the user can simply write the words right after summoning the program. So if the program is in a file called *wordfreq.icn* one might write

icont wordfreq.icn -x the by in

to translate and execute the program for those three words. Later we shall show how we can proceed if the user fails to enter one or more words. The main procedure is quite simple:

```
procedure main(word_list)
  process(get_valid_filename, word_list)
end
```

The first argument of process() is obtained just as before. The second, which is the user's word list must be passed on to process() which otherwise would know nothing about it. As an alternative, one could specify a global variable right at the very beginning of the program (wl let us say) and assign word_list to this variable. Then all procedures can use it. In this procedure we shall use a structure called a table. This resembles a list, but the various elements instead of being referenced by integers may be referenced by any data object—strings, for example. We set up our table by

```
word_table := table(0)
```

If at this stage we check the value of, let us say, word_table["the"], it will return 0, but this does not mean that there is actually such a value in the table. The length of the table (found by word_table) is zero. Once some value is assigned to an element in the table the element comes into being, and the length of the table is increased by one. So

```
word_table["the"] +:= 1
```

increases the *the*-th element by one. Tables make it very easy to tabulate numbers related to strings. Additionally both the values and the indexes of tables can very easily be sorted into order, alphabetical or otherwise. We shall therefore use getword() to bring in the words from the file. Each individual word will be checked against each word in the list furnished by the user. If a match is found, the corresponding entry in the table will be incremented, and looking for further matches will cease. It should be pointed out that while this method of word checking works, it is cumbersome and tedious. A better method, more in the spirit of Icon, involving pattern matching will be discussed in the next chapter. When we are through we shall move to another procedure which will print out the results on the screen in alphabetical order. Here is the procedure:

```
procedure process(filename, word_list)
local filvar, counter, word, n, word_freq
#set up the frequency table
  word_freq := table(0)
#open the previously checked file
  filvar := open(filename)
#initialize the word counter
  counter := 0
#bring out the words in the file one at a time
  every word := getword(filvar) do {
#increment the word counter
    counter +:= 1
#check the word against the user's list
    every n := 1 to word_list do
      if word == word_list[n] then {
#if found increment the corresponding slot
#in the table
        word_freq[word] +:= 1
#and break out of the inner loop - no point
#in further checks
        break}}
#close the file, pass the counter and the
#table to printout
  close(filvar)
  printout(counter, word_freq)
end

procedure printout(c, wf)
local wl,n
  write; write; write
  write("Total number of words in file= ",c)
  writes("Word")
  writes(right("Occurrences",30))
  writes(right("Percentage",30)
#sort the table into a list
  wl := sort(wf)
#print list
  every n:= 1 to wl do {
    writes(wl[n][1])
    writes(right(wl[n][2],30))
    writes(right((wl[n][2] * c) / 100.0,30))}
end
```

You will note that the function **sort()** takes a table and creates from it a list. This list itself contains a group of lists in which the first element is the entry in the table and the second is the value of the entry, the entries now being in order. So in the preceding program **wl[3][1]** refers to the third sorted entry in the table (now a list), while **wl[5][2]** refers to the value of the fifth sorted entry. There is an alternate way of handling this. If you add *3* as the second argument of **sort()** then a single long list will be created in which the entries and values of the tables will alternate, the entries being in sorted order. Try modifying the preceding program to use this feature. The second argument *2* will produce a list in which there is a group of lists sorted according to value rather than entry, and the second argument *4* will produce a single list in which entries and values alternate, but sorting is by value rather than entry. The function **sort()** may also be used to sort lists, in which case the order of items is simply rearranged. No second argument is available for sorting lists. Numbers will be sorted before strings. It should be noted that sorting is according to the order in the computer character set, so all uppercase letters will occur before all lowercase letters.

SUMMARY OF ICON FEATURES

1. In the line-scanning facility the position of the imaginary pointer at any time is stored in the keyword **&pos**. The line which is being scanned is stored in the keyword **&subject**.

2. Positions in the line may be numbered positively from the left (beginning at 1) or negatively from the right (beginning at 0).

3. The function **pos()** succeeds if the argument (positive or negative) corresponds to the position of the pointer in the line being scanned.

4. Exponentiation is expressed by the caret ($\wedge$). On some keyboards this character may appear as the up-arrow ($\uparrow$) or circumflex ($\char"005E$). Roots may be obtained by a fractional exponent. The following comparisons would succeed:

$$(7 \wedge 2) = 49$$

$$(16 \wedge 0.5) = 4$$

5. The tilde ($\sim$) is used to negate an operator such as equals ($\sim$=). It is not to be confused with **not** which negates conditional expressions, making them succeed when they would fail and vice versa.

6. The function **table()** creates a structure in which values may be indexed by any data object. Its argument becomes the initial value of each element in the table.

7. The function **sort()** will accept a table as its argument and produce a sorted list as its result. With no second argument this will be a list of two-element lists, the first element being an entry from the table and the second its value, the entries being in order. If the second argument is *2*, sorting is by value. If the second argument is *3* or *4*, a single list is created in which entries and values alternate, sorting being by entry (*3*) or value (*4*). Lists may also be sorted. Numbers will be sorted before strings, which are arranged in character set order.

8
Correlation

8.1 THE SPEARMAN RANK CORRELATION COEFFICIENT

In this section we shall develop a program to figure the Spearman Rank correlation coefficient. It is set up as though dealing with a correlation between the date of composition of plays and the average number of words per verse indicating a constant increase or decrease, but it could of course be used for many other purposes with slight modification. It is assumed that the values of words per verse will be read in order of date of composition. The values could be read in random order, provided that they were associated with some value that would rank them.

Here is a table of the information for ten plays of Corneille:

Date	Mean Words per Verse
1629	8.93
1632	9.02
1635	9.147
1640	9.26
1644	9.152
1650	9.2
1662	9.22
1666	9.32
1672	9.48
1674	9.53

Let us first decide to give the user the option of giving the values on the line which calls the program or is being solicited for them by the program. We can achieve this with a main procedure as follows:

```
#Calculates Spearman Rank Correlation Coefficient

procedure main(command_line)
#if the command line has data send it to process,
#otherwise let get_info() get it.
  if *command_line = 0 then
    process(get_info()) else
      process(command_line)
end
```

Here the main procedure has a parameter command_line. If the user writes values after the instruction to the computer to call the program, these values will be stored in command_line in the form of a list. So we measure the length of the list. If it equals zero, then the list is empty, and we call a procedure get_info which will solicit the missing information and return it as its value. This can then be supplied to the procedure process() which will do the main work of the program. Otherwise we simply supply what we got in the command line to process().

Now let us see how get_info() will function. We have to get the values into a list to replace command_line which the user left empty, so we will set up a variable dlist. Since we do not know how long the list will be, it will be best to set it up empty and allow it to expand to be as large as necessary. We achieve this by

```
dlist := list(0)
```

which creates a list of zero length. This function may take a second argument which gives an initial value to each element of the list, but that would be pointless in this instance. Alternatively we may write

```
dlist := []
```

which serves the same purpose. The square brackets enclose the list, and here they are enclosing an empty list. Now Icon has a function

```
put()
```

which puts the value of its second argument at the tail of the list that is its first argument. For example

```
put(dlist,1.5)
```

would make 1.5 the first element of dlist. Executing subsequently

```
put(dlist,2.0)
```

would make 2.0 the second element of **dlist** and so on. Notice that the elements are added at the *right* side of the list, that is, at its tail. We are actually creating an entity called a *queue*, because if subsequently we come to process the list from left to right, we shall meet first with the first element that was put in. We may think of it as a theater queue or line; the first person to come is the first to get a ticket. This is sometimes known by the acronym FIFO—first in, first out. We may mention in passing that there is a similar function **push( )**, which adds an element to a list on the *left* side, so that if we process from left to right, the last element to go in is met with first. This is known as LIFO—last in, first out—and creates an entity called a *stack*, which may be compared to a stack of dishes; when you get one you use the one that was placed there last. So

```
put(dlist,read())
```

will add to the right of **dlist** whatever the user types in at the keyboard. We want to repeat this as many times as the user desires.

```
while put(dlist,read())
```

will keep on doing this so long as **put( )** succeeds. But how can we get it to stop? There is no way that the computer can read the mind of the user, and know that a particular value is the last. (Compare this with the situation where a disk file is being read, and the computer finds a physical "end of file.") Now Icon has a function

```
numeric()
```

which converts its argument to a whole number (integer) or number with a decimal point (real number) *if possible*. If it is not possible it will fail. So

```
numeric(read())
```

will succeed if **read( )** is bringing in numbers and fail otherwise. (We may note that when we type in **1.5** for instance we are really entering a string which at some point Icon will automatically convert to a real number. Here we are doing the conversion *explicitly* to achieve a particular effect.) All we need to do is to instruct the user to enter some nonnumeric data (a period point, for example). The function **numeric( )** will then fail, and **put( )** will be "infected" by this failure and fail too. So the loop will end. This will serve the additional purpose of excluding bad data; as soon as something other than a number is entered, no further data will be accepted. For safety's sake it will be a good idea to repeat back to the user the data that the program is working with so that any discrepancy can be noted. One final point. What if the user enters no data even when solicited, either just hitting return or entering a period immediately? It might be well to check if this has happened (by measuring the length of the list) and stop the program if it has. Otherwise we may be doing calculations with no data. In addition, a significant aspect of the "user-friendliness" of a program is its capacity to handle bad data appropriately, by making a new request for good data, or bringing the program to an orderly halt, without the benefit of cryptic messages from Icon or the operating system. It is worth noting that we have not really attempted to check what the user puts in if the command line is used. Perhaps we can assume that a user doing that will be extra careful; perhaps we should indeed devise some checks for that method too, but we shall not do that here. You may want to consider how that might be done. (The list could be scanned to see what is in it before processing it, for example.)

Our procedure now appears as follows:

```
procedure get_info()
local dlist
  dlist := []
  write("Enter mean words per verse fo_
    r each play in order of composition.")
  write("Hit return after each value.  Sin_
    gle period + return to finish.")
#add values to list at right end
  while put(dlist, numeric(read()))
  if *dlist = 0 then stop("Bye!")
return dlist
end
```

We now proceed as follows with procedure process(drama_list) which will do the actual calculation of the coefficient. The parameter of the procedure will hold the list of values which the user has provided, and have been entered in chronological order by year. We can sort this into ascending order very easily by the Icon function sort() which takes a list as its argument and returns the sorted list as its value. So

```
sort_list := sort(drama_list)
```

gives us a list of the same length as drama_list with the values in order. Now let us set up a table in which the indices are the *values* of sort_list and the values are the *position* of each value in sort_list. This is achieved by

```
dtable := table(0)
every n := 1 to *drama_list do
  dtable[sort_list[n]] := n
```

Be sure to understand this step; the value in **sort_list** becomes the index in **dtable**, and the current position, represented by **n**, becomes the value of that element of the table.

We now have to create a sum of the squares of the difference between each item's rank on the two scales. One scale is already ranked and is represented by a constantly incremented **n**. The other is represented by

```
dtable[drama_list[n]]
```

The index to **drama_list** returns a value which, when passed to **dtable** returns the ranking in the sorted version of the list. Note the manner in which an indexed variable (**drama_list[n]**) can be the index of another variable (**dtable[ ]**). Having previously initialized a variable **sum_of_squares** to 0, we proceed to increment it by the new value squared:

```
every n := 1 to *drama_list do
    sum_of_squares +:= ((n - dtable[drama_list[n]]) ^ 2)
```

(We used a circumflex here. It is the same character as the wedge used in the next statement.)

Now we are ready to calculate the coefficient known as **rho** (ρ):

```
rho := (1 - (6 * sum_of_squares) / (real(*drama_list) *
    ((*drama_list ∧ 2) - 1)))
```

This can all be written on one long line even though it is wider than the screen. Icon accepts statements even though they are too long for the screen. If you do break it, do so at a point where the line is clearly unfinished, after an addition sign, for example. The value is then written to the screen. It is often desirable to use real numbers in division in order to ensure that remainders are not discarded by integer division. Converting one of the values to a real number by **real()** ensures this.

The complete procedure now looks as follows:

```
procedure process(drama_list)
local sort_list, sum_of_squares, n, dtable, rho
#initialize sum_of_squares and n
  n := sum_of_squares := 0
#sort the list
  sort_list := sort(drama_list)
#create a table of locations from sort_list
  dtable := table(0)
  write("Values are:")
  while write(drama_list[n +:= 1])
  every n := 1 to *drama_list do
    dtable[sort_list[n]] := n
#figure the differences and sum the squares
  every n := 1 to *drama_list do
    sum_of_squares +:= ((n - dtable[drama_list[n]]) ^ 2)
  rho := (1 - (6 * sum_of_squares) / (real(*drama_list) *
    ((*drama_list ^ 2) - 1)))
  write("rho = ",rho)
return
end
```

8.2 SCATTERGRAMS

The scattergram indicates visually whether there is a correlation between two sets of variables, and is often a useful precursor to the coefficient just mentioned in order to see if it is worth pursuing.

Clearly we can have a program in which the same data is used to figure the Spearman coefficient and draw a scattergram, but we will do it rather differently here in order to illustrate some features of Icon that have not occurred before. You may want to consider developing an integrated program which does both. Let us set up a main procedure like this:

```
procedure main()
  get_values()
  figure()
  scatter()
end
```

The program is in three parts. One obtains the necessary data; one manipulates the data so that it can be used; and one puts the dots that constitute the scattergram on the screen. It is necessary to get the data in pairs, so we will allow the user to enter any amount of values, but the total must be even. It is not possible then to allow the user to enter a period at any time; it must

be done only for one value of the pair. For this purpose a **repeat** loop may
be useful. Unlike **while** which iterates so long as the control expression at
the top succeeds, and **every** which iterates so long as the control expression
at the top produces a result, **repeat** goes on forever. It has no control expression. It may be stopped by the expression **break**, and this is what we in
fact do:

```
procedure get_values()
   values := []
   repeat {
     writes("X-value?  Nonnumeric to finish.  ")
     put(values,numeric(read())) | break
     writes("Y-value?  ")
     while not put(values,numeric(read())) do
        writes("You must enter a numeric value.  Y-value?  ")}
return
end
```

We first initialize the variable **values** to the empty list and then enter the
repeat loop, using the curly bracket to warn Icon that all the following commands until the corresponding curly bracket are to be considered part of the
loop. We first solicit the x-value from the user, and check that it is numeric.
If it is, we put it in the list of values. If it is not, we break out of the loop, and
the collection of data is done. The symbol | means *or* and implies that if the
expression preceding it fails, then the one following should be tried—*either*
put the value in the list *or* break out of the loop. This statement is equivalent
to:

```
if not put(values,numeric(read())) then break
```

but it is more concise and easier to understand. Once the user has put in
an x-value, then a y-value *must* be put in. So we set up a loop (inside the
repeat loop) which is entered only if the user attempts to exit at that point by
entering a nonnumeric. This will recur until a proper value is entered, and the
repeat loop starts over. This time we shall not return **values** as the value of
the procedure. **values** will be declared a global variable which is accessible to
all procedures in the program. As we mentioned already, variables of this type
should be used sparingly. Since they can be altered anywhere in the program,
they are prone to cause errors which are difficult to detect. Where possible,
keep variables local, using them only in one procedure. The declaration of
global variables must be done right at the beginning of the program thus:

```
global values
```

These paired values must now be placed on a grid on the screen. How
can we do this? The easiest, although not the only, way to do this is to move

the cursor around the screen directly to the point concerned. Most terminals are capable of doing this, but the instructions may vary to achieve the
necessary effects. The illustration given here is for the IBM PC or compati-
bles. It may require consultation with your terminal manual to find what the
corresponding commands are for your terminal.

First we have to note that some kind of scaling is necessary. The text
screen has 25 lines (the x-axis) and 80 columns (the y-axis). It is also possible
to have a 25 × 40 screen. There are graphic screens on which points can
be plotted with great accuracy, but these are not accessible to the current
implemention of Icon. For this purpose we shall need to know the range of
our data, and adapt it to the size of the grid which we have available. We
will therefore declare the variables for the minimum values of x and y and the
range of x and y as global variables. The maximum value will not be further
needed and so may be declared a local variable in **procedure figure()**. The
very first line in our program now looks like this:

```
global values, x_min, x_range, y_min, y_range
```

We are now going to run through the values supplied by the user and
determine the minima and maxima. We first set both **x_min** and **x_max** to
the first value, since at this point this value is both the maximum and the
minimum. We do the same for the **y** value. Since we have already taken care
of the first two values we can start looking at value three. We set a variable
n to 3, and are going to increment it in steps of two, since the **x** and **y** values
alternate. We now have a pair of or-statements:

```
(x_min := (x_min > values[n])) |
  (x_max := (x_max < values[n]))
(y_min := (y_min > values[n + 1])) |
  (y_max := (y_max < values[n + 1]))}
```

Let us consider the **x** statement first. We are going to try to assign a value
to **x_min**. If we succeed, then we shall skip the "or" part of the line. If we
fail, we shall try to assign something to **x_max**. In other words, if we find a
value of **x** lower than the current minimum, it will replace that minimum. If
that does not work, we shall check if it can replace the maximum. Of course,
both attempts may fail. The expression

```
x_min > values[n]
```

succeeds if the value of **x_min** so far is greater than the current element in
values, and returns the second value—i.e., that of values[n]—and this then
replaces the former minimum. We cannot use the more natural expression

```
values[n] < x_min
```

because then **x_min** would be returned, and no change would take place. There is no intrinsic reason for returning the second value; it is a decision made by those who constructed the language. When the loop finishes, we have ascertained the maximum and minimum values for the x- and y-axes. From these we can calculate the range, and then go on to scale these to fit the screen. Our procedure now reads as follows:

```
procedure figure()
local x_max, y_max, n
  x_min := x_max := values[1]
  y_min := y_max := values[2]
  every n := 3 to *values by 2 do {
    (x_min := (x_min > values[n])) | (x_max :=
      (x_max < values[n]))
    (y_min := (y_min > values[n + 1])) | (y_max :=
      (y_max < values[n + 1]))}
  x_range := x_max - x_min
  y_range := y_max - y_min
end
```

(For the sake of illustration we broke the long line in a different place here, ending the first part in a place where it is clearly incomplete.) The procedure for scaling is quite simple. We pass to it the particular value we wish to scale:

```
procedure scale(n,min,range,max)
return integer((n - min) / real(range) * max)
end
```

and it returns the scaled value.

We can regard our screen as a grid numbered from 1 to 25 vertically and 1 to 80 horizontally. Executing a **writes()** statement

```
writes("\e[1;1H")
```

moves the cursor to the top left corner of the screen, but writes nothing there.

```
writes("\e[25;80H")
```

moves the cursor to the bottom right corner. It is permissible to write this statement in pieces, provided that we do not separate the \e which represents the escape character. If the value of q is 25 and of **trh** 80 then an equivalent statement to the last is

```
writes("\e[",q,";",trh,"H")
```

This feature enables us to *compute* the coordinates. The cursor is then sent to the computed coordinates, and a dot is printed there. Here is the complete program, including the procedure to place the dots appropriately on the screen:

```
global values, x_min, x_range, y_min, y_range

procedure main()
  get_values()
  figure()
  scatter()
end


procedure get_values()
  values := []
  repeat {
    writes("X-value?  Nonnumeric to finish.  ")
    put(values,numeric(read())) | break
    writes("Y-value?  ")
    while not put(values,numeric(read())) do
      writes("You must enter a numeric value.  Y-value?  ")}
  return
end


procedure figure()
local x_max, y_max, n
  x_min := x_max := values[1]
  y_min := y_max := values[2]
  every n := 3 to *values by 2 do {
    (x_min := (x_min > values[n])) |
      (x_max := (x_max < values[n]))
    (y_min := (y_min > values[n + 1])) |
      (y_max := (y_max < values[n + 1]))}
  x_range := x_max - x_min
  y_range := y_max - y_min
end


procedure scale(n,min,range,max)
return integer((n - min) / real(range) * max )
end
```

```
procedure scatter()
local n
  writes("\e[2J")
  every n := 1 to *values by 2 do {
    writes("\e[",26 - ((scale(values[n +
      1],y_min,y_range,24) + 1)),
        ";",scale(values[n],x_min,x_range,79) + 1,"H")
    writes(".")}
end
```

SUMMARY OF ICON FEATURES

1. The main procedure may have have a single argument. Then, if the program is called with following arguments these will be stored in the form of a list in the variable constituting the argument of the main procedure.

2. list(i,x) creates a list of i values with the initial value of x.

3. put(l,x) adds the value x to the right of the list l.

4. numeric(n) returns a numeric value for n if it can, and fails otherwise.

5. repeat initiates a "perpetual" loop concluded by break.

9

Pearson's Coefficient of Correlation

9.1 PLANNING THE PROGRAM

In this chapter we shall develop a program to calculate Pearson's coefficient for word frequency in two texts. Kenny comments as follows (p. 83):

> Calculation of the Pearson product-moment coefficient by means of its definition formula can be a slow and laborious business, since it involves calculating the mean and standard deviation for each of the two distributions involved, and the conversion of all the values along each scale into z-scores. This will have become apparent to the reader on working through even the artificially simple exercises in the text...

Kenny goes on to point out that hand calculators often include a routine for calculating the coefficient. This program offers the possibility of calculating the coefficient easily, once the texts or a sample of them are available in machine-readable form—and preparing these is much less tedious and error prone than working through texts by hand and making the calculations. Additionally, it seems likely that optical scanners which are able to convert printed matter, or even written matter, into machine-readable form will become much cheaper and more readily available. Readers are already available which can read different styles and sizes of type.

Let us now consider what information we shall need, and how we shall proceed. From the user we shall need three pieces of information: a set of words, the occurrence of which is to be checked in the texts, and the names of two files which contain the texts. Our main procedure will call a procedure to get the set of words, and use twice the procedure to get a valid filename which we have used before. The results of these three procedures will be passed to a procedure which will systematically use this information to calculate the coefficient. Our main procedure then will look like this:

```
procedure main()
  process(get_words(),get_valid_filename(),
    get_valid_filename())
end
```

The second and third arguments of `process()` give the user three chances to designate a valid filename, and end the program if this effort does not succeed. The first one will get a list of words, and we can also use it to explain the program. The three pieces of information are passed to **procedure process()** which will do the main work of the program. If we wish to make the main procedure less succinct but more readable we can use three local variables thus:

```
procedure main()
local word_list,filename_1,filename_2
  word_list := get_words()
  filename_1 := get_valid_filename()
  filename_2 := get_valid_filename()
  process(word_list,filename_1,filename_2)
end
```

Both of these approaches are valid, and which one chooses is a matter of style. The procedure `process()` will proceed as follows:

1. Create a table for file *A* in which the index will be the words concerned, and the values will be the number of times the word occurs. This table will be created by another procedure which will get the words from the file (using a procedure we have used before) and compare them with the word list.

2. Create a similar table for file *B*. These tables will not necessarily be the same length, since some words may occur in only one file.

3. For ease of processing, convert both tables to lists of values in the same order. From this point on we do not need to know what the word is; we have to have paired values for the two files. The two lists will be in corresponding order.

4. Figure the mean of the values of file *A*, using a procedure for that purpose, then do the same for file *B*.

5. On the basis of step 4, figure the standard deviation for each text, using a procedure similar to one already used, but quite general this time.

6. On the basis of step 5, figure the z-score for each pair of values in the lists derived from the tables, multiply them together, and keep a running total.

7. The coefficient is figured by dividing the running total by the length of the word list, and is printed on the screen.

9.2 GETTING INFORMATION FROM THE USER

Here is the procedure which will give the user some information, and also request some.

```
procedure get_words()
local word,word_list
  word_list := []
  write(); write(); write()
  write(center("PEARSON PRODUCT-MOMENT COEFFICIENT",64))
  write(center("------- ------- ------ -----------",64))
  write()
  write("This program will figure the co_
     efficient for a set of words")
  write("you will supply as they oc_
     cur in two texts.  Enter them one")
  write("at a time, following each by press_
     ing Return.  When you are")
  write("through enter a single per_
     iod and press Return.  You will be")
  write("asked twice for an in_
     put file.  Enter valid file names.")
  write("Please enter the words.")
  while (word := read()) ~== "." do
     put(word_list,word)
return word_list
end
```

This procedure is quite simple. It has only two local variables: **word** which will hold the words as they come in from the user, and **word_list** into which the individual words will be placed and will ultimately be returned as the value of the procedure. We start by initializing **word_list** to an empty list, and then write some instructions to the screen. These could be formatted in any way you find esthetically pleasing; the function **center()** is helpful in doing this, and a little experimentation will indicate what works best. It is a good idea to start with clearing the screen, but how this is done depends on your particular terminal. It will normally involve writing some code to the screen. This will usually be a control character or some characters beginning with the escape character which is used to indicate that what follows are not the usual printing characters. For the ansi system of MS-DOS and some others, the following should work:

```
writes("\e[2J")
```

This is the *escape* character, represented in Icon by \e followed by a code arbitrarily set by the system. If this does not work, look in the manual for your terminal for the appropriate code for *clear screen* or *home and clear*— or ask someone who might know! The user then types in a word at a time, following each by return. The end of the list is signalled by entering a single period or some other appropriate character. Our loop then is

```
while (word := read()) ~== "." do
   put(word_list,word)
```

that is, so long as the word read is *not* a single period enter the loop which adds the word to the word list. Note that the item read is assigned to word, and it is the value of that assignment operation which is checked against a single period before the loop is entered. The possible length of the list is limited only by the computer's memory; it is unlikely that this will present a problem with a list of reasonable size. As soon as the loop is concluded the word list is returned as the value of the procedure, and this is in turn passed by the main procedure to a procedure which will process the information. Two final points before we leave getwords(). First,

```
word_list := list(0)
```

would be an acceptable alternative for initializing word_list. Second, it might be a good idea before returning the word list to check that it actually contains something; the user might have entered a period immediately. We could do this by checking if the length of the list is zero, in which case we stop the program:

```
if *word_list = 0 then stop("Bye!")
```

9.3   FIGURING THE COEFFICIENT

The procedure which we shall call process() will have the three arguments mentioned before, and a number of local variables. If the local variables are too many to place conveniently on one line we can repeat the word local.

For each of the two files we shall need variables to contain a table, a list, a mean, and a standard variation. In addition we shall need a variable to contain the running z-score product and finally one for the coefficient we are seeking. Here is the procedure:

```
procedure process(wl,fnm_a,fnm_b)
local table_a,table_b,list_a,list_b,n,a_mean,b_mean
local a_sd,b_sd,z_sc_product,coefficient
  z_sc_product := 0
  table_a := make_table(fnm_a,wl)
  table_b := make_table(fnm_b,wl)
  list_a := list(*wl,0)
  list_b := list(*wl,0)
  every n := 1 to *wl do {
    list_a[n] := table_a[wl[n]]
    list_b[n] := table_b[wl[n]]}
  a_mean := mean(list_a)
  b_mean := mean(list_b)
  a_sd := st_dv(a_mean,list_a)
  b_sd := st_dv(b_mean,list_b)
  every n := 1 to *wl do
    z_sc_product +:= z_sc(list_a[n],a_mean,a_sd) *
      z_sc(list_b[n],b_mean,b_sd)
  coefficient := z_sc_product / *wl
  write()
  write("Coefficient is ",coefficient)
end
```

We initialize the running z-score product to 0. Then we create a table for each file, using a procedure which we shall discuss soon. We then create a list for each file, which has as many elements as there are words in the word list, and the initial value of which is 0 in each case. We then make each word in the word list in turn the index of the table, and transfer the value to the new list. Notice that if a value is missing in the table because the word did not occur in the file, it will still return the value 0, and this will be entered in the list as an actual value. We then figure the means and the standard deviations; from this the sum of the products of the pairs of z-scores and then the coefficient. We now have to consider the procedures that contribute to this procedure.

9.4 CREATING THE TABLE—PATTERN MATCHING

In order to create a table, we must get the words in turn from the file (which we already know how to do) and then compare them with the words in the word list, incrementing the appropriate entry in the table if a match is found. On a previous occasion we did a similar operation by using a loop which compares each word in turn with the members of the word list and jumps out if a match is made. Icon has a much better way of doing this kind of operation. In order to understand it we must examine the nature of the string scanning facility in Icon. When this facility is invoked by following the string, or string valued variable, by the question mark, two keywords are activated. &subject contains the original string that is being processed. &pos contains the position of the imaginary pointer which moves along the line as we process it, and is initially set to 1; that is, immediately left of the first character in the string. Both &subject and &pos are global; that is to say, both can be accessed by any other procedure. Accordingly it is possible to set up a procedure outside the one in which the string scanning facility is in operation which will utilize these keywords and give back information to the string scanning operation. Here is our procedure to make a table:

```
procedure make_table(flnm,l)
local t
  t := table(0)
  every word := getword(flnm) do
    word ?  if is_in_list(l) then
      t[word] +:= 1
return t
end
```

This procedure creates a table of which the initial values will all be 0. We then get one word at a time from the file, call up the scanning facility for that word, and determine if the word is in the list. If it is, the corresponding index has its value incremented by one. The procedure is_in_list() will succeed only if the word which is the subject of scanning is in the list provided to is_in_list as its argument.

9.5   MATCHING AGAINST A LIST OF WORDS

For our purposes we can use a procedure referred to by Griswold (p. 161) slightly modified.

```
procedure is_in_list(l)
suspend tab(match(!l)) & pos(0)
end
```

The exclamation point prefixed to a variable produces the elements of that variable in turn. For example, if l is a file, it will produce each line in the file, and we could use an **every** loop to print out those lines or use them in some other way. In this case, **l** is a list. Now **suspend** which returns a result and leaves the procedure intact rather than departing from it entirely as **return** does, acts like **every** inasmuch as it prompts the production of every possible result. So what happens is as follows. Let us assume that the words in the word list are *he she we you* and the word against which we are matching them is *weed*. The expression **!l** first produces *he* and **match()** attempts to find this string starting at the current position of the pointer which is 1. **match()** fails and so **tab()** fails too. (Since this combination of **tab()** and **match()** is so common, Icon possess a shorthand notation for it which consists of placing the equal sign before the string or the string valued variable.) **!l** now produces *she* which meets with the same fate. When *we* is produced **match()** succeeds and returns 3, which is the position in *weed* after the string *we*. **tab()** now moves the pointer up to position 3. So far we have a positive result. This is conjoined by **&** with the result of **pos(0)**. However, this fails, since the pointer is not at the end, and the whole procedure fails. Since this scanning operation is complete however, the original position of the pointer at the beginning is restored, and another try is made with *you* which fails in the same way as the first two. If the word against which we are matching is *we* rather than *weed*, the third attempt will succeed and so the procedure will succeed since it is producing a result. This is not strictly a "matching procedure" as Icon defines it, since the matching procedure should produce the string between the original and the ultimate position of the pointer. However, in this case our interest is purely in a yes-no answer to the match, as we already have the string in which we are interested.

Here now is our complete program. Comments have been added. The procedures for computing in turn the mean, the standard deviation, and the z-scores should be self-explanatory.

```
#This program solicits a set of words and two
#filenames containing texts. It calculates Pearson's
#coefficient of correlation for the frequency of
#the words in the two texts.

procedure main()
  process(get_words(),get_valid_filename(),
    get_valid_filename())
end

#For each text make a table, the index
#of which is a word, and the value of
#which is the number of occurrences.
#Convert this info to a list of values
#for each text. Figure the mean, standard
#deviation, and thence the z-scores for the
```

```
#raw scores, and figure coefficient based
#on pairs of scores.




procedure process(wl,fnm_a,fnm_b)
local table_a,table_b,list_a,list_b,n,a_mean,b_mean
local a_sd,b_sd,z_sc_product,coefficient
  z_sc_product := 0
  table_a := make_table(fnm_a,wl)
  table_b := make_table(fnm_b,wl)
  list_a := list(*wl,0)
  list_b := list(*wl,0)
  every n := 1 to *wl do {
    list_a[n] := table_a[wl[n]]
    list_b[n] := table_b[wl[n]]}
  a_mean := mean(list_a)
  b_mean := mean(list_b)
  a_sd := st_dv(a_mean,list_a)
  b_sd := st_dv(b_mean,list_b)
  every n := 1 to *wl do
    z_sc_product +:= z_sc(list_a[n],a_mean,a_sd) *
      z_sc(list_b[n],b_mean,b_sd)
  coefficient := z_sc_product / *wl
  write()
  write("Coefficient is ",coefficient)
end




#Gives instructions & solicits word list from user




procedure get_words()
local word,word_list
  word_list := []
  write(); write(); write()
  write(center("PEARSON PRODUCT-MOMENT COEFFICIENT",64))
  write(center("------- ------- ------ -----------",64))
  write()
```

```
      write("This program will figure the co_
        efficient for a set of words")
      write("you will supply as they oc_
        cur in two texts.  Enter them one")
      write("at a time, following each by press_
        ing Return.  When you are")
      write("through enter a single per_
        iod and press Return.  You will be")
      write("asked twice for an in_
        put file.  Enter valid file names.")
      write("Please enter the words.")
      while (word := read()) ~== "." do
        put(word_list,word)
    return word_list
    end
```

```
#Gives user three chances to enter a valid filename
```

```
    procedure get_valid_filename()
    local filename
      every 1 to 3 do {
        writes("What is the name of the input file?  ")
        filename := read()
        if close(open(filename)) then {
          write("OK")
          return filename} else
        write("Unable to open file.")}
      stop("Bye!")
    end
```

```
#Figures the mean of a list of values
```

```
    procedure mean(l)
    local total,n
      total := 0
      every n := 1 to *l do
        total +:= l[n]
    return real(total) / *l
    end
```

```
#Figures the standard deviation of a list of values
#based on mean
```

```
procedure st_dv(m,l)
local sum_of_squares,n
  sum_of_squares := 0
  every n := 1 to *l do
    sum_of_squares +:= ((l[n] - m) ∧ 2)
return (real(sum_of_squares) / *l) ∧ 0.5
end
```

#Figures the z-score based on raw score, mean,
#and standard deviation

```
procedure z_sc(raw_score,m,sd)
return (raw_score - m) / real(sd)
end
```

#Succeeds if the subject matches
#any of a list of words

```
procedure is_in_list(l)
  suspend =!l & pos(0)
end
```

#Creates a table of occurrences of
#list of words from a file

```
procedure make_table(flnm,l)
local t
  t := table(0)
  every word := getword(flnm) do
    word ?  if is_in_list(l) then
      t[word] +:= 1
return t
end
```

#This procedure produces one word at a time from the
#file. Definition of word is somewhat primitive.

```
procedure getword(filename)
local chars, punct, filvar, line, word
  chars := (&lcase ++ &ucase ++ '1234567890\'-')
  punct := ' .,?";:!'
  filvar := open(filename)
```

```
    while line := read(filvar) do
      line ?  {tab(many(' ')) #skip leading blanks
        while word := tab(many(chars)) do {
          tab(many(punct))
          suspend word}}
    close(filvar)
  end
```

9.6 MORE ON MATCHING

Let us now consider a further possibility of using Icon's ability to match strings. You will recall that in order to figure the Pearson coefficient we need three pieces of information from the user:

1. The name of the file containing Text A.

2. The name of the file containing Text B.

3. A set of words, the occurrence of which is to be checked in the texts.

Let us assume now that instead of getting this information interactively as we have done using prompts, we shall allow the user to enter this information on the command line, making the assumption that the first two valid filenames on the line are the names of the files concerned, and all the other entries are the words that are going to be checked. Note that this time we are not checking that the file *exists*; we may indeed wish to check that also, but here we are checking that the actual name of the file follows appropriate rules as to how it is spelled out. We could incorporate this feature into the main procedure by checking to see if the list coming in from the command line contains anything; if it does we use it, if not, we solicit the information interactively as before. For our purpose, a valid filename will be from one to eight of the characters permitted by MS-DOS followed by a period followed by the ending *txt*, which is called the *extension*, and usually consists of three letters which hint at what the file contains. For example, a file containing a document may have the extension *doc*, while one containing an Icon program must end in *icn*. Your system may have different rules for filenames which you should check locally. For example, the following are valid filenames for MS-DOS, and follow the rules we just set up for ourselves:

- mill.txt

- mill#1.txt

- Jackson.txt

- James(5).txt

These are invalid:

- mill?.txt (MS-DOS forbids "?")

- mill.tex (wrong extension)

- millicent.txt (too long)

- Jackson (no extension)

For the moment we shall write a separate program which will simply take a list of strings from its command line, identify the two files, and print them out. We shall do this by taking the command line (which is a list of strings) and turning it over to a procedure which will return and print out a list of two strings that meet our needs if it finds them. If we wanted to use this technique in the preceding program, we could put the filenames into one list, the words for matching in another, place both lists in another list, and return it as the value of the procedure. This information can then be passed to `procedure process()`.

Here is our main procedure:

```
procedure main(command_list)
local filelist
  filelist := getfiles(command_list)
  write("First file is ",filelist[1])
  write("Second file is ",filelist[2])
end
```

The procedure `getfiles()` will return a list of up to two files, and store it in `filelist`. The `write()` commands will only be followed if the appropriate element in `filelist` exists, since the attempt to retrieve the contents of an element ([1] or [2] in this case) will fail if that element does not exist, and that failure will be "inherited" by `write()`.

In `getfiles()` we shall proceed something like this:

- Prepare an empty list which will hold the valid filenames.

- Bring in a word from the command line list.

- If a procedure gives the OK, add it to the new list.

- Quit when two valid filenames have been found, or the old list ends.

Let us now convert this to Icon language. The first preceding item becomes:

```
l_out := []
```

We now need a loop to bring in each string from the command line in turn. Let us assume that in this procedure the command line has been stored in l.

```
every n := 1 to *l do
```

Now we invoke the string scan:

```
l[n] ? if isfile() then put(l_out,l[n])
```

The procedure `isfile()` will succeed if l[n] is indeed a valid filename, and then it will be added to the new list. Otherwise we go on to try a new string. There is one additional thing. Once we have found two files, we should like to stop, and we can achieve that by setting up a flag. After the first file is found, the flag goes up; when the second is found the flag is checked, found to be up, and the procedure stops. Now if we establish a variable **flag**, its initial value is null. This we take to be the flag in its down condition. We can check this by prefixing a frontslash (/) to the variable. This will produce the variable **flag** if that variable is null; otherwise it will fail. So the command

```
/flag := "up"
```

will *succeed* the first time it is met with in the program, since the value of **flag** is null; however the value **"up"** will be assigned to **flag** which is produced by the expression **/flag**. Accordingly, the next time around

```
/flag := "up"
```

will *fail* because now **flag** *does* have a value, and is not null. You will notice that **/flag** produces a *variable* not a value, and it is this fact that allows a new value to be assigned to **flag**. Of course, we don't have to use the string "up". The arbitrary number 1 would do equally well. There is a similar prefix, the backslash (\), which succeeds if the variable it precedes does have a value. Finally we may note that an expression like **if flag then**... is useless, since it will always succeed, producing null or some value, and being successful in either case. Using this feature our procedure becomes:

```
procedure getfiles(l)
local l_out,n,flag
  l_out := []
  every n := 1 to *l do
    l[n] ? if isfile() then {
      put(l_out,l[n])
      (/flag := 1) | break}
return l_out
end
```

Since the **flag** statement fails the second time around, the alternative following the bar is taken account of, and the loop stops at the behest of **break**. The flag statement is put into parentheses to make sure it is properly grouped. Now we reach the crux of our discussion: the procedure **isfile()**.

We first declare a static variable **mschar**. By declaring **mschar** as **static** it will retain its value however many times the procedure is called. There is then a command preceded by the word **initial** which means that it will be done only the first time the procedure is called. This avoids unnecessary computation of a value that will never change. This stores in **mschar** a set of all the valid characters for filenames. The function **many()** will then span all such characters and return the position immediately after the last of them. **many()** must find at least one character to succeed; so by including **10 > ** at the beginning of the expression we exclude the possibility of more than eight letters, since such string of eight letters would return 9 (the position after the eighth letter) and this is the highest number that will fulfill the proviso that 10 is greater than it; if any higher number occurs, the expression will fail, and so the whole line will fail. We then need to find a period followed by *txt* at which point the string must end. This is expressed by

```
tab(match(".txt"))
```

where **match()** looks for the string that is its argument immediately after the imaginary pointer, and **tab()** then moves the pointer beyond it. The equal sign may be used also thus:

```
=".txt"
```

The end of the string is symbolized by conjoining the **pos(0)** function, which ensures that the pointer is now at the end. So we have:

```
procedure isfile()
static mschar
initial mschar := &ucase ++ &lcase ++
  '1234567890$&#%\'()-@∧ {}~'!_'
return tab(10 > many(mschar)) || =".txt" & pos(0)
end
```

Should we wish **txt** to be permissible in any of the eight possible combinations of lower- and uppercase letters we might substitute

```
="." || tab(any('Tt')) || tab(any('Xx')) ||
  tab(any('Tt')) & pos(0)
```

The function **any()** will look for a single character in its argument immediately after the current position of the pointer, and return the position after it. An alternative way to handle this, since MS-DOS does not distinguish between upper- and lowercase in filenames, would be to convert each name first for matching purposes to a single case:

```
procedure upcase(str)
return map(str,&lcase,&ucase)
end
```

will take any string as its argument and will return a similar string with any lowercase letters converted to uppercase letters. The function map() makes a one for one replacement in its first argument of the letters in the corresponding places of the strings which are the second and third arguments. In this case the keywords represent character sets which are automatically converted to strings for this purpose. If we would reverse the second and third arguments, it would produce a string with no uppercase letters.

You may wish to try modifying the program for figuring the coefficient to allow an option of providing the information in the command line. You will need an if-statement in the main procedure such that an empty command line triggers the interactive solicitation of information, and a command line with information is processed such that the filenames and wordlist are correctly passed to process().

9.7 SETS

Icon has another structure which can often be fruitfully used in matching words. We have previously learned something about character sets or "csets" which are created in Icon by placing a group of characters between single quotes and are useful with such functions as upto() which looks for a point in the string where any member of the cset occurs. Icon can handle sets of items other than single characters. Set theory is a branch of mathematics that was elaborated by Georg Cantor, and a brief example will help explicate the kinds of situations in which it can be helpful. Let us imagine that committee A has as its members Jones, Brown, Rodriguez, and Sperber while committee B has as its members Robinson, Schwartz, Rodriguez, and Sperber. If the two committees meet together, the joint committee will have a membership of six and not eight. If we take away from the joint committee those members who only belong to one committee, a set of two persons will be left. Icon is able to mirror operations of this type. In order to create a set we start with a list

```
["Jones","Brown","Rodriguez","Sperber"]
```

and convert it to a set by the function set():

```
committee_A := set(["Jones","Brown","Rodriguez","Sperber"])
```

Note that an identical individual item that recurs in the list will occur only once in the set, and unlike the list, the members of the set are in no particular order. We can check if an item is a member of a set by the function `member()`. So in this instance

```
member(committee_A,"Jones")
```

would succeed and return the value "Jones". If the second argument had been "Schwartz" the function would have failed. This can readily be used to check the occurrences of a wordlist in a text. We set up a table to hold the occurrences of particular words:

```
wordcount := table(0)
```

and a set of the words we are checking

```
wordlist := set(["you","we","they"])
```

then as each word comes in and is stored in the variable **word** the statement

```
wordcount[member(wordlist,word)] +:= 1
```

will create a table in which the entries are the members of the set (or as many of them as occur in the text) and the values are the number of occurrences. No if-statement is required. If the word is not in the set, the function `member()` will fail and no assignment will be made, since the entire statement will fail. If it is in the set, it is returned as the value of `member()` and becomes the index of the table. The value of that entry is then increased by one. The length of the table will be as many entries as have been found at least once, but if a nonoccurring word is checked in the table it will return 0, since that is the initial value of table entries. This is a good example of how the useful Icon structures table and set can be used to produce concise code in which a single line does a great deal of work.

The equality of two Icon sets can be checked by a triple equal sign (`===`). We have already met the single sign being used for the equality of numbers and the double sign being used for the equality of strings. A member can be inserted in a set as follows:

```
insert(committee_A,"Jackson")
```

or we could put Jackson in his own set and unify the two.

```
committee_A ++:= set(["Jackson"])
```

Set union and difference is shown by the double plus sign or minus sign, and set intersection (which gives the set of members that belong to both) by the double asterisk. In the just-cited example `committee_A` and the new set are unified, and the result is assigned to committee_A which now has the new value of the combined sets. The function delete(committee_A,"Jackson") would remove Jackson from the set. Both insert() and delete() always succeed and cannot be used to check to see if a member is there or not; for this member() must be used.

SUMMARY OF ICON FEATURES

1. An empty list may be created by list(0) or a pair of empty square brackets([]).

2. The word local declaring the names of variables may occur more than once.

3. &subject and &pos are global keywords (accessible to all procedures). The first contains the string being scanned. The second contains the current position of the pointer used in string scanning.

4. The exclamation point (!) prefixed to a variable produces the elements of that variable.

5. The equal sign (=) prefixed to a string or string-valued variable is equivalent to tab(match()).

6. The ampersand (&) conjoins statements so that both must succeed for the whole to succeed. The bar (|) alternates statements such that if one succeeds, subsequent ones are not evaluated, and the whole succeeds.

7. The frontslash (/) prefixed to a variable succeeds and produces the variable if its value is null (the initial value of variables.) The backslash (\) prefixed to a variable succeeds and produces the variable if its value is something other than null. Otherwise it fails. A variable without either always succeeds because it always produces something.

8. If the Icon main procedure has a variable as its argument, that variable will contain a list valued at the strings written after the command that calls the program. So if the first line of the main procedure is procedure main(c) and the line calling the program is *coefficient he she it*, then c will be a three-string list consisting of "he", "she", and "it".

9. An attempt to access a list element that does not exist will cause failure (which will be "inherited" by any procedure calls in which such attempt occurs).

10. A variable declared **static** will retain its value from one call of the procedure to the next providing "memory" for the procedure. A statement (or compound statement inside curly brackets) preceded by the word **initial** will be executed on the first call of the procedure only. Statements like this must occur at the beginning of the procedure.

11. The double bar (||) concatenates (joins together) strings.

12. The function **map()** makes a one-for-one replacement in its first argument of the letters in the corresponding places of the strings which are the second and third arguments.

10
Programming a Nursery Rhyme

10.1 TEN GREEN BOTTLES

In this chapter we shall try to generate some rhymes, both as an exercise in becoming sensitive to structures in language and to learn some new Icon features.

The structure of the rhyme "Ten Green Bottles" is fairly obvious. It is a loop in which the number constantly decreases until it reaches zero—a rather fancy description of a child's rhyme. We need to set a variable to 10, decrease its value by one each time a bottle falls, and come out of the loop when 0 is reached:

```
procedure rhyme()
local n
  n := 10
  while n > 0 do {
    write(n," green bottles hanging on the wall.")
    write(n," green bottles hanging on the wall.")
    write("Now if 1 green bottle should accident_
      ally fall,")
    write("There'd be ",n -:= 1," green bottles hang_
      ing on the wall.")}
end
```

The symbols -:= written together decrease the value of the variable by what follows just as +:= increase it. A quoted string may be broken up for convenience between lines by using an underscore to denote that a continuation is to be expected. Now we just need to call this procedure and it will print out the entire rhyme. There are, however, some inelegant features occasioned by the conventions of the English language which we may wish to remove. First, we are supposed to spell out small numbers and not use the numeral. There is no automatic connection in Icon between "1" and "one". The first is a one-character string representing an integer, a counting number, and the second is a three-character string which is the name in English of that integer. The first item may change according to the number system ("I" in the Roman and "א" in the Hebrew system, for example), while the second may change according to language ("uno" in Spanish or "één" in Dutch), but they always point to the same underlying integer. We might make this connection by setting up a list with ten elements and then fill it with the appropriate words:

```
numbers := list(10)
numbers[1] := "One"
numbers[2] := "Two"
```

and so on.

If this procedure were going to be called more than once it would be appropriate to declare **numbers** as **static** rather than **local** and initialize the elements in **numbers** in a compound **initial** statement (i.e., **initial** followed by the assignments inside curly brackets) since their value will never change. It is unthinkable that the string "Two" could ever be assigned to **numbers[1]** for instance. By declaring the variable as static and designating the statements as initial, the assignments are made once for all and retained from one call of the procedure to another. In this case it makes little difference, since the procedure is only called once. You might like to try writing a procedure that will return the name in English, or some other language, when furnished with an integer between 1 and 100. How would you avoid spelling out the numbers between the tens greater than twenty? (Hint: Remember the modulo—%.)

We still have a problem in that we have not allowed for zero. Actually, if we run the program like this the last line will not be written because the attempt to access **numbers[0]** will fail, and so the **write()** will fail too. Then we can add the missing line after the loop. We begin by initializing the index to 10, and then enter the loop:

```
n:= 10
while n > 0 do {
   write(numbers[n]," green bottles hanging on the wall.")
   write(numbers[n]," green bottles hanging on the wall.")
   write("Now if one green bottle should accidentally fall,")
```

```
    write("There'd be ",numbers[n -:= 1]," green bottles hang_
        ing on the wall.")}
write("There'd be no green bottles hanging on the wall.")
```

Notice how the indentation shows that the last command is outside the loop. By moving the line back we show that the flow of the program has moved up one level, and is not inside the loop. An alternative approach would be to use a table instead of a list. Then we could have a 0 index also.

The conventions of English are giving us some new problems. We wrote in the numbers with capital letters, but the third line requires a small letter. So we can set up a procedure to take care of this:

```
procedure lcase(s)
return map(s,&ucase,&lcase)
end
```

This is a general procedure that takes a string and turns any uppercase letter into the corresponding lowercase letter, leaving everything else unchanged. So now we have

```
    write("There'd be ",lcase(numbers[n -:= 1])," green bot_
        tles hanging on the wall.")}
```

Bearing in mind that write() writes to the screen all its arguments in order, notice what the second argument of write() does. It decreases the value of n by one, then uses the value of the assignment statement as the index of a list which produces a string which is then converted to all lowercase letters. There is one other inelegant feature. When we get to "one", "bottle" does not need an s. (Curiously, with "no" it does!). We can, of course, avoid the issue by writing "bottle(s)" in the first instance, but somehow this seems in order for an official form but inappropriate for a nursery rhyme. Spelling out for a computer all the feelings and intuitions we have with respect to our own language is a truly enormous task. We can cope with this by setting up a procedure for plurals that will return s or a null string according to circumstances:

```
procedure plural(n)
local s
  s := "s"
  if n = 1 then s := ""
return s
end
```

Giving a variable a certain value and then promptly changing it if some particular condition is true is often a clearer formulation than an else-leg on the if-statement, namely

```
if n = 1 then s:= "" else s := "s"
```

Notice too the way the null string is used. It regularizes the situation such that each word ends in something—even if that something is invisible! Here now is the complete program:

```
procedure main()
  rhyme()
end

procedure rhyme()
local n,numbers
  n := 10
  numbers := list(10)
  numbers[1]  := "One"
  numbers[2]  := "Two"
  numbers[3]  := "Three"
  numbers[4]  := "Four"
  numbers[5]  := "Five"
  numbers[6]  := "Six"
  numbers[7]  := "Seven"
  numbers[8]  := "Eight"
  numbers[9]  := "Nine"
  numbers[10] := "Ten"
  while n > 0 do {
    write(numbers[n]," green bot_
      tle",plural(n)," hanging on the wall.")
    write(numbers[n]," green bot_
      tle",plural(n)," hanging on the wall.")
    write("Now if one green bot_
      tle should accidentally fall,")
    write("There'd be ",lcase(numbers[n -:= 1]))," green bot_
      tle",plural(n)," hanging on the wall.")}
  write("There'd be no green bot_
    tles hanging on the wall.")
end

procedure plural(n)
local s
  s := "s"
  if n = 1 then s := ""
return s
end
```

```
procedure lcase(s)
return map(s,&ucase,&lcase)
end
```

Two observations may be made on this program. First, it is generally not worthwhile to program small items. Once one gets beyond a very crude product, considerable work goes into programming, especially where natural language is concerned. Programming is most efficient when large amounts of data are to be processed, or the program can be used over and over on small amounts of data. For this reason it is hardly worthwhile to write a program to balance a checkbook, while in contrast word processors, which get a great deal of use, have been very successful. Second, this little program illustrates the *explicitness* that programming requires. Many human beings can be trusted to perform a task intelligently, making intuitive allowances for special circumstances. The computer must be told precisely what to do, without ambiguity. Dealing with natural language is particularly troublesome in this regard, since it has many ambiguous and unexpected features which are hard to anticipate. It is this fact which has made progress in machine translation from one natural language to another much slower than was initially expected.

10.2 THE HOUSE THAT JACK BUILT

If we examine the structure of the nursery rhyme called "This is the House that Jack Built" we shall see that it consists of two loops, one within the other. The outer loop constantly brings in two new elements, a noun or noun phrase and a verb or verb phrase, while the inner loop trots out all the previous nouns and verbs, so that the verses get progressively longer. To get started we need two nouns and a verb which are then set in a particular framework, then subsequently we need only one noun and one verb which are set in a slightly different framework, but this pattern repeats indefinitely. Accordingly it will be well to have a procedure to get us going and generate the first phrase, and then pass this to a procedure which will generate the rest of the rhyme:

```
procedure get_started()
local str
  writes("This is the ")
  str := read()
  writes("That ")
  str ||:= " that " || read()
return str
end
```

This procedure has one local variable which will hold the string which will ultimately be the last few words of each verse. We prompt the user to enter "house" (or an equivalent) by printing out the words: "This is the " and staying on the same line. Note the blank at the end of this phrase; this makes it unneccesary for the user to insert one. The function `writes()` does this for us since it does not issue a carriage return. This is stored in `str`. We then print "That " at the beginning of the next line to solicit "Jack built." or the equivalent. This is added to the previous string along with the word " that " (surrounded by spaces). The symbols `||:=` increase the string by what follows just as `+:=` do with integers. At this point we might want to consider simply continuing to make the string longer each time in the same way. This is possible, since we can even include carriage returns in the string. For this we use `\n` (for *newline*). Thus the string

```
"this is a \ntest"
```

would print out

this is a

test

(There are some other so-called "escape" characters of this type. `\l` is exactly the same as `\n`. This stands for *linefeed*, which is the ASCII name for this character. The previous symbol is the newer UNIX terminology for the same character. `\r` brings the cursor back to the beginning of the line and in effect overwrites what is there already. This is a simple carriage return without the linefeed which normally accompanies it. `\b` is a backspace.) However, it is not a good idea to create very long strings, even though it can be done. Long strings are clumsy to manipulate, and the string would have *the* and *that* repeated many times, using up storage space unnecessarily.

Let us observe first of all that in each repetition of the rhyme the words inserted later are mentioned earlier, "last in, first out." This arrangement is typical of the *stack* (like the restaurant plates) and is represented by a list which uses `push()` to push new elements in at the *front* (the left side) of the list. There is also a function `pop()` for *removing* an element from the left side of the list, but since Jack is cumulative we do not need to use it. It will be best to set up a stack for nouns and a stack for verbs, adding the new "plates" to the stack as they come in.

```
procedure rhyme(conc)
local noun,verb,nouns,verbs,n
  nouns := []
  verbs := []
  repeat {
    n := 0
    write()
    writes("This is the ")
    noun := read()
    writes("That ")
    verb := read()
    writes("The ")
    while write(nouns[n +:= 1]) do
      writes("That ",verbs[n]," the ")
    push(nouns,noun)
    push(verbs,verb)
    write(conc)}
end
```

Since the rhyme can theoretically go on forever, the outer loop is well represented by **repeat** which goes on indefinitely. Two stacks (empty lists) are created. At the beginning of the loop, an index variable is initialized to zero. The noun and verb are then solicited from the reader and stored in variables. The inner loop then looks for the first noun, and since the index is being constantly increased by 1, the loop will finish when it exhausts the stack, by trying to access an element that will not exist until the next time around. The first time the loop will not even be entered, since it will try to access an element (nouns[1]) which does not yet exist. When this loop finishes, the string which was created by the previous procedure is printed out. We add the new items to their respective stacks, and the repeat loop is ready to start again. The entire program now looks like this:

```
procedure main()
  rhyme(get_started())
end

procedure get_started()
local str
  writes("This is the ")
  str := read()
  writes("That ")
  str ||:= " that " || read()
return str
end
```

```
procedure rhyme(conc)
local noun,verb,nouns,verbs,n
  nouns := []
  verbs := []
  repeat {
    n := 0
    write()
    writes("This is the ")
    noun := read()
    writes("That ")
    verb := read()
    writes("The ")
    while write(nouns[n +:= 1]) do
      writes("That ",verbs[n]," the ")
    push(nouns,noun)
    push(verbs,verb)
    write(conc)}
end
```

It would be possible to use only one stack, keeping both verbs and nouns on it in pairs. You might like to modify the program to use this approach.

10.3   RANDOMIZING JACK

We can have a little fun with this rhyme by shuffling the stack with the result that we may find the malt biting the house and other improbable and amusing combinations. We can achieve this with a procedure mentioned in Griswold (p. 97) which they use initially for strings, but works equally well for lists. In order to understand the procedure, we need to consider two useful Icon features that we have not met before. The question mark (?) prefixed to a variable produces a random element of that variable, if, like a list, it contains various elements. Do not confuse this with the question mark that invokes the scanning facility. That is a *binary operator* which is surrounded by spaces and connects the two expressions on either side. The one we are speaking of is a *unary operator* which affects only the variable it precedes. If the variable is valued at a whole number greater than 0, it will produce a random number between one and that whole number. If the variable is valued at 0, it will produce a real number somewhere between zero and one. The other Icon feature in this procedure is as follows. You will recall that the expression

```
x := y
```

assigns the value of y to x. Icon has an exchange operator :=:. So

```
x :=:  y
```

assigns the value of y to x, and the value of x to y. The two variables exchange
values. Now let us look at the procedure.

```
procedure shuffle(l)
local i
  i := *l
  while i >= 2 do {
    l[?i] :=:  l[i]
    i -:= 1}
return l
end
```

The local variable is set to the size of the list. Let us say there are eight
elements, so the value of i will be 8. We then enter a loop in which an
element selected at random will be exchanged for the last element in the list,
number 8. The value of the local variable is then decreased by 1, so the
exchange is with the last but one element, and this will be a string selected
from the first seven elements. When the number of the variable drops below
two the loop finishes, because no exchange is possible when only one element
is involved. So

```
shuffle(nouns)
```

will randomly rearrange the various elements in nouns. But how shall we
activate this shuffling? An easy way would be to invite the user to add some
character (say a plus sign) to any answer. We then check each answer to see
if a plus sign is there. If it is, we shuffle the stack and delete the plus sign
so that we are left with a regular word. Since this will be done in a separate
procedure, we need to make the two stacks global, so that the new procedure
can operate on them. While it is a good idea in general to avoid global
variables, in this case it would be clumsy to pass the information between
procedures. While we are about it, we may as well give the user some way
of concluding the program (since Jack is potentially infinite) let us say by
entering a period in the answer, and arrange to use the same procedure for
shuffling two different stacks. This can be achieved by an extra argument
that indicates whether nouns or verbs are to be shuffled. The following will
achieve what we wish:

```
procedure check(s,n)
local p
  if upto('.',s) then stop()
  if p := upto('+',s) then { s[p] := ""
    if n = 1 then shuffle(nouns) else
      shuffle(verbs)}
return s
end
```

The procedure **check()** first looks for a period. If it finds one, the program ends. A string can appear as an argument of **stop()**, a commercial for a local builder let us say, which is printed on the screen before the program ends. Here **upto()** is being used outside of the string scanning facility, and so the string it is operating on must be specified as the second argument. Other string scanning functions may be used similarly. You may like to try modifying the program so that the string scanning facility is used in this case too. If no period is found, a check is made for a plus sign. If no plus sign is found, the procedure simply returns the original string unchanged. If a plus sign is found, it is first eliminated from the string. Strings can be indexed, so if the value of **str** is "steak" then the value of **str[2]** is "t". New values can be assigned to such indexed variables, and the size of the string changes automatically. So

```
str[2] := "tr"
```

would change "steak" to "streak" and

```
str[1] := ""
```

would change it to "teak". This last method is used to eliminate the plus sign which has now served its purpose. The procedure then checks the second argument. If it finds a "1" it scrambles the nouns; otherwise it scrambles the verbs. The original word, stripped of its plus sign, is now returned as the value of the function. To incorporate this in the program we just replace both occurrences of **read()** in procedure **rhyme()** by **check(read(),1)** and **check(read(),2)**.

As an exercise you may like to try adding the possibility of *un*scrambling the stacks. To do this we need to set up two more stacks (we might call them **nouns_bak** and **verbs_bak**) which are filled at the same time as the regular stacks but are not affected by **shuffle()**. Then, when the user inserts some other symbol which **check()** can recognize, the scrambled stack is replaced entirely by the backup stack:

```
nouns := copy(nouns_bak)
```

The function **copy()** when used with lists, tables, and records creates an exact but *distinct* copy. If this were omitted, both **nouns** and **nouns_bak** would reference the same list, and the program would not work properly. This is why in 10.3 we did not need

```
nouns := shuffle(nouns)
```

Normally, when you pass an item to a procedure a copy of it is made, but this does not apply to lists, tables, and records (known collectively as "structures") where the actual item is accessed. Three versions of this program are on the accompanying disk (113.ICN, 116.ICN, and 117.ICN). Try to understand one before proceeding to the next.

SUMMARY OF ICON FEATURES

1. The combination of symbols -:= decreases the variable on the left by the value on the right.

2. The combination of symbols ||:= concatenates the string variable on the left to the string or string variable on the right and assigns the result to the variable on the left.

3. It is permissible to break a string between lines if the first part of the string is followed immediately by an underscore.

4. The following "escape" characters may be used in strings:

   \n or \l newline

   \b backspace

   \r return to beginning of line

   Also, you may precede \, ' and " by the backslash if you want them to represent themselves literally and not the special functions they normally fulfill as marker or delineator.

5. Strings may be indexed to access individual characters in the string. Such indexed characters may have other values assigned to them, and the length of the string is automatically adjusted.

6. The function **copy()** makes a distinct copy of tables, lists, and records. In other cases it simply produces the value, and so the result is not different from the result of the original item.

11
Creating a Data Base

11.1 A GRADE PROGRAM

In this chapter we shall consider the possibility of establishing a data base, which is one of the most useful features that the computer has for many users along with word processing programs and spread sheets. Despite horror stories of unfortunate sufferers who are dunned to pay up zero dollars, computers have made record keeping much simpler, at least when they are properly programmed and used. While many excellent commercial data base programs are available for general and specialized applications, it will be helpful to write a simple program of this type in order to see what it can do. Possibilities exist for research as well as practical purposes. Care must be employed in this kind of endeavor since security becomes important, both in terms of not losing crucial data and of avoiding snooping or tampering by third parties. The latter is a complex issue which will not be dealt with here. Some systems include a program which will encrypt a file which cannot then be used until it is decrypted by means of a password. If you need this kind of security, you may want to check what is available on your system, or you may be able to obtain a program to keep your files secret. On time-sharing systems it is normally possible to make files private so that others cannot read them. The UNIX system has a program *chmod* which can make a file available only to its owner, and you can check the documentation to learn how to use this program. It should be pointed out that Icon keeps its records in ASCII which is useful insofar as the files can be read by an editor or an operating system command to "list" the file (i.e., print it out—the term comes from the days when program source files with commands that could be listed were the only files written in something like natural language). But it

119

also means that unauthorized access is easier. Some programming languages create binary data files that can only be read by a program designed to do so. Building a simple data base will also give us the opportunity to use the Icon feature called *record*. In Icon the list is a very flexible structure which may expand and contract in length, be added to or subtracted from at either end, and hold varying types of data. The result of this is that the record is not quite as useful in Icon as it is in some languages where the data structures corresponding to the list (arrays, for example) are more restricted in their use. The record resembles a list in that its elements can be accessed by a numerical index. It resembles a table in that its elements can be accessed by name. It differs from both in that the names of its elements and hence its length are predetermined. The nature of the record has to be declared at the beginning of the program, and may be used by all procedures in the program which are not allowed to have their own individual record declarations. Note that the declaration of a record at the beginning of a program does not *create* a record. It specifies rather the attributes of the record variable when it comes to be created in the course of the program. It is useful when we have an item that has various fixed attributes that are interesting to us, for example, age, sex, address, telephone number, and so on.

It would be possible to write a program simply to figure student grades, but that is rather trivial and better achieved with a pocket calculator. More significant is a program which will preserve information, can use that information to generate new information, can be updated from time to time, and can issue some kind of report. The techniques covered here can be used for many other data base applications.

In the first instance our program will have three sections:

- Initialization. This makes it possible to enter and preserve information that may reasonably not be expected to change: name, address, date of birth, and so on. Of course, someone can marry and change names or move, but we may disregard this for the moment.

- Updating. This makes it possible to enter information that was not initially available, such as the results of tests or assignments.

- Reporting. This makes it possible to retrieve the information that has been entered, perhaps after some calculations or other manipulations that make the data more useful.

The features which might be added to these are virtually infinite, as are the enhancements that might be added to these sections. We might want to bring in the use of a printer, perhaps for different types of reports. We will certainly wish to emend as well as update, dropping or adding students, for example. We may wish to make the files generated by the program available to another program, for example, one which would enable an individual student to access a restricted set of information of particular relevance. It is also desirable to add protections against the entry of inappropriate information, and help in case the user should need it. These last two items make the program "user-friendly." Above all, the program should be able to accept enhancements and modifications easily, so that the aforementioned three sections could be expanded to five, or twenty-five, simply by adding more procedures.

Our main program will call a procedure to get initial information from the user, and on that basis call the appropriate procedure:

```
procedure main()
local result
  result := menu()
  case result of {
    "1" :  initialize()
    "2" :  update()
    "3" :  report()
    default :  write("Goodbye")}
end

procedure menu()
  write(center("Data Base Program",80))
  write()
  write("Do you wish to")
  write("\t1.  Initialize")
  write("\t2.  Update")
  write("\t3.  Report")
  write()
  writes("Enter 1, 2 or 3 and press return.  ")
return read()
end
```

The main procedure calls a procedure **menu** and stores the value of that procedure in **result**. Let us look at **menu()**. It prints out the name of the program and offers a "menu" of three options. The menu is a common way to offer options to the user. You may have a numbered list of the options, and invite the user to enter the appropriate number. An alternative method is to invite the user to press an arrow key and then the cursor moves between the various alternatives on the screen. In order to implement the second possibility, you need to know what character is sent to the computer by the arrow keys (different keyboards may have different conventions), and then when the program detects this character it moves the cursor appropriately, accepting the information from the user when finally the return key is pressed. Since the first method is easier to implement and less dependent on local conditions, we shall stick to that one. The \t is an Icon character that represents a horizontal tab, giving the effect here of a small indentation. The procedure menu() returns whatever the user types in, without running any checks on the validity of the answer. Now the main procedure takes this value, and submits it to a case statement. A case statement allows for a multiple choice condition. The value that is being checked (here, result) appears between the words **case** and **of**. This is followed by a curly bracket and a set of lines divided by colons, which are checked through in order. If the value of **response** corresponds to the left-hand part of the first line, then the rest of the line after the colon is executed, and the program continues after the closing curly bracket of the case statement. If it does not correspond, then the next is tried and so on until the curly bracket is reached. It is possible to use the word **default**, which is executed if all else fails. The statement containing **default** is always tried last, wherever it occurs in the case statement, so you could put it first, if you wish, to emphasize the default. Note that "1", "2", and "3" come in as strings (as does everything from the keyboard) and must be checked as strings. Icon frequently makes automatic conversions of data. But in this case there is simply a comparison, and so the items must belong to the same data type to be considered identical. The main procedure simply shunts the flow to the appropriate procedure, or shuts down with a polite farewell if it is unable to do so. You may like to try modifying the program to allow more chances to the user. It is a little more difficult here than before, but it should be possible to find a way to do it.

Even at this early stage it is possible to check to see if the program is working. Add some dummy procedures as indicated next, and then give it a try:

```
procedure initialize()
  write("Space reserved for initialization.")
end

procedure update()
  write("Space reserved for updates.")
end

procedure report()
  write("Space reserved for reports.")
end
```

After we see that the basic flow is correct we can replace the dummies with procedures that actually do some work. Let us look first at initialize(). At the beginning of the program we must place a record declaration which gives the name of the record type (we shall call it students) and has as its arguments the names of the various elements which it contains. Here is the record declaration, placed first in the program:

```
record students(name,soc_sec,pwd,fstexam,
  secexam,final,total,grade)
```

and here is the procedure for initialization:

```
procedure initialize()
local filename,student,student_table,student_list
  student_table := table()
  writes("Enter the course number, e.g.  101 ")
  filename := read()
  writes("Enter the last two digits of the current year ")
  filename ||:= read()
  writes("Enter a single digit for the semester ")
  filename ||:= read() || "1.dat"
  writes("The name of the file is ",filename)
  write(".  Please note this for future use.")
  write("Enter information about students.  Enter per_
    iod(.)  when asked for name to finish.")
  repeat {
    student := students("","","",0,0,0,0,"")
    write()
    writes("Name?  ")
    student.name := read()
    if student.name == "." then break
    writes("Social security number?  ")
    student.soc_sec := read()
    writes("Password?  ")
    student.pwd := read()
    student_table[student.name] := student}
  student_list := sort(student_table)
  write_to_file(filename,student_list)
end
```

We need a file in which to keep our information. We could simply ask the user to designate a filename, but here we construct a filename from the course number, year, and semester (which amounts to six digits) and then add a 1 (which will be increased for each update file) and the extension *.dat*. We then ask the user to note this name as the identification of this particular series of information. In this manner a series of files will be created automatically. The way we shall do it will work properly for nine files only. You may wish to consider how to modify the program to make it work for ninety-nine files, which should be possible without too much difficulty. We then enter a loop to structure the incoming information appropriately. We initialize a variable **student** as a record of the type of **students**. The initial values are zero for numerical items and the empty string for string items. We then fill in such information as we can. We do not even ask for the score on the first examination for example, and that stays at the 0 to which it was initialized. A password of the student's choosing is entered in case we wish to make the scores available on a limited basis to individuals possessing the password to their particular entry. Observe that the particular element of the record is accessed by placing a dot after the record variable and then the name of the element. This is much more understandable in this case than using a list, which is referenced only by numbers. We then place the information in a table indexed by the name. This preserves the information and enables us to reinitialize the record variable and use it for the next student. Additionally, it will be easy to alphabetize the list later using the Icon **sort** facility. The loop then starts over. Anytime a single period is detected in the first entry, the loop terminates. This kind of loop is used because it is necessary to reinitialize the variable each time, and this is not a suitable item to control a while loop. Actually a while loop could be used, and is in fact a more "structured" solution. Initialize the variable *before* entering the loop, and use the first reading of information to control the loop:

```
while (student.name := read()) ~== "." do {
```

This reads in the student's name and then uses the *value* of the assignment statement to check that it is not a period, in which case the loop will finish. Then we have to reinitialize the record variable at the *bottom* of the loop, right after placing the information in the table. This means that the initialization of the record variable is written twice: once outside the loop and once inside.

The table is then sorted. This converts the table into a list which itself contains a set of lists equal in number to the items in the table. The first item in each of these lists is the index of the table. The second item is the value of the table. These lists will appear in the order of the ASCII character set according to the index, now the first item in each list. (You can also sort by the value if you wish, by adding *2* as the second argument in the **sort()** function.) We pass this information and the filename to **write_to_file** which will write out the information to the file and can be used by the other procedures for the same purpose. Here it is:

```
procedure write_to_file(f,s)
local filvar,n,p,line
  filvar := open(f,"w")
  n := 0
  while (n +:= 1) <= *s do {
    line := ""
    every p := 1 to 8 do
      line ||:= s[n][2][p] || "%"
    write(filvar,line)}
  close(filvar)
end
```

This procedure first opens the file to which it will write the information. The second argument `"w"` permits writing to the file. If this is omitted the file can be read only. Two loops are used to get the information in the student list into a format suitable for the ASCII file. The outer loop keeps going as many times as there are students which is indicated by the length of the student file. The inner loop runs eight times specifically since there are eight pieces of information on each student. The inner loop will first look at the first item of the second element (which is a record) of the first list, and start off a line with it. It will add a percent sign as a divider, then look at the second item of the second element of the first list and add this to the line. After eight times of doing this, it will write the line to the file, reinitialize the line to the empty string and then look at the first item of the second element of the second list, and so on until all students and their attributes have been recorded. We now have the information filed in a consistent manner.

Let us talk a little about the structures that are involved here. The student list is a list that itself consists of lists, as many as there are students in the class. Each of these lists has a fixed number of elements, namely 2. The first element is the name, and the second element is a record, which contains information relevant to the student. The format has been dictated by the manner in which the table sort in Icon works, and hence there is a duplication of the name. But it is convenient to keep this format, because anytime we wish we can easily use the sort facility again, for example, if we would later add new names. This is a nested structure—wheels within wheels. Icon cannot write such a nested structure to a file. We have to write it in a sequential fashion, using some arbitrary symbol as a marker between the different fields. When we bring back in the information from the file, we can restore it to its nested form that is convenient to work with when manipulating the information. Note that when we want to process all the information in the record, it is often convenient to index the record as though it is a list of fixed length, rather than referring to the elements by name.

Let us now consider a procedure to update the information. It will do this in a rather gross fashion, offering the user all the current information and giving the opportunity to enter the same information or to change it. You may wish to consider making this more specific, perhaps by offering a menu. Another possibility is to allow the original score to stand by allowing an empty string (which the user enters simply by pressing return) to represent the same score as before.

We first have to get the name of the current file, and we do this by asking the user for the original name, then constructing a name with the version number that that name contains constantly being increased until failure indicates that such a file does not yet exist:

```
procedure get_version()
local filename,n
  n := 0
  write("Enter the name of the ORIGINAL filename ")
  filename := read()
  while close(open(filename[1:7] || (n +:= 1) || ".dat"))
return filename[1:7] || (n - 1) || ".dat"
end
```

Note that this assumes that none of the old files have been deleted, and allows for only eight updates. We now take this file, put the information back into the original structure, solicit replacement entries from the user, and then write out the new information to the next file in the series. A typical filename might be 2058713.dat where the 205 would be the course number, the 87 would be the year, the 1 would be the semester and the 3 would be the sequential number of the version, increased from the original 1. filename[1:7] produces the section of filename between positions 1 and 7, i.e., the first six characters of the string. Such ranges of parts of a string-valued variable may also be negative, starting from 0 for the position **after** the last character in the string and then counting back -1, -2, and so on. So filename[-1:0] would produce the last character in the string. The Icon line scanning facility is used to detect the percent sign in the file used as a marker, and the field between the old and new positions of the pointer is stored in each element of the record. We skip over the percent sign by ="%". The command move(1) would have the same effect in this case. Here is the procedure:

```
procedure update()
local filename,filvar,n,student_list,line,student,
  inner_list,current
  filename := get_version()
  filvar := open(filename)
  student_list := [ ]
```

```
while line := read(filvar) do {
  student := students("","","",0,0,0,0,"")
  inner_list := list(2)
  n := 0
  line ?  while student[n +:= 1] := tab(upto("%")) do
    ="%"
  inner_list[1] := student.name
  inner_list[2] := student
  put(student_list,inner_list)}
close(filvar)
n := 0
while current := student_list[n +:= 1][2] do {
  write("Name:  ",current.name)
  write("Current first exam = ",current.fstexam)
  writes("New score?  ")
  current.fstexam := read()
  write("Current second exam = ",current.secexam)
  writes("New score?  ")
  current.secexam := read()
  write("Current final exam = ",current.final)
  writes("New score?  ")
  current.final := read()
  student_list[n][2] := current}
filename[7] +:= 1
write_to_file(filename,student_list)
end
```

The current file is first opened, and read using the file variable **filvar**. The variable **student_list** is initialized to an empty list, and we shall push on to it as many inner lists as there are students in the class. We initialize **inner_list** to a list of two elements, the first of which is to contain the student's name, and the second the student's record. From the first line we extract all the items and place them in a record variable which reproduces the original form of the record. When complete, this is placed in the second item of the inner list, and the name only in the first item. This is then pushed onto the student list, as just indicated. This is repeated for as many students as there are in the class. Our original nested structure has now been reproduced. The second part of the procedure extracts each record in this nested structure, stores it temporarily in a variable **current**, and uses this to display and maybe change the information. Since **current** is being used as a record, it is possible to add a period and the respective record field to it. When we are through, the same procedure as before is used to write the information to the new file.

We shall leave it to the reader to write a report procedure. This might take the exam scores and sum them, perhaps with some scaling, such as 40% for the final and 30% for the other exams. This figure will be stored in the total element of the record. The grade might be figured by a long if-statement:

```
if current.total >= 92 then current.grade := "A" else
if current.total >= 89 then current.grade := "A-" else
```

and so on. It is not necessary to state the range of the grade. As soon as it is found to be greater than or equal to one of the stated numbers, it gives a value to **current.grade** and skips out of the if-statement. Note that as one of the if-statements fits, then all the rest are skipped because they form part of the else-leg of that particular statement. The end will be something like:

```
if current.total >= 64 then current.grade := "D-" else
current.grade := "F"
```

The final **else** picks up all that remains, which is in effect any grade below 64.

You may wish to try writing a program for a student to access only one record. This will involve having the student enter a password. This will be compared with the password field on each line, and if a match is found make accessible the rest of the data on that line. This program is offered for illustration only, and no guarantees are given as to its effectiveness in practice.

Here now is the program at the point to which it has been developed:

```
record students(name,soc_sec,pwd,fstexam,
  secexam,final,total, grade)

procedure main()
local result
  result := menu()
  case result of {
    "1" :  initialize()
    "2" :  update()
    "3" :  report()
    default :  write("Goodbye")}
end

procedure menu()
  write(center("Data Base Program",80))
  write()
  write("Do you wish to")
```

```
     write("\t1.  Initialize")
     write("\t2.  Update")
     write("\t3.  Report")
     write()
     writes("Enter 1,2 or 3 and press return.  ")
  return read()
  end

  procedure initialize()
  local filename,student,student_table,student_list
     student_table := table()
     writes("Enter the course number, e.g.  101 ")
     filename := read()
     writes("Enter the last two digits of the current year ")
     filename ||:= read()
     writes("Enter a single digit for the semester ")
     filename ||:= read() || "1.dat"
     writes("The name of the file is ",filename)
     write(".  Please note this for future use.")
     write("Enter information about students.  Enter per_
        iod(.)  when asked for name to finish.")
     repeat {
        student := students("","","",0,0,0,0,"")
        write()
        writes("Name?  ")
        student.name := read()
        if student.name == "." then break
        writes("Social security number?  ")
        student.soc_sec := read()
        writes("Password?  ")
        student.pwd := read()
        student_table[student.name] := student}
     student_list := sort(student_table)
     write_to_file(filename,student_list)
  end
```

```
procedure write_to_file(f,s)
local filvar,n,p,line
  filvar := open(f,"w")
  n := 0
  while (n +:= 1) <= *s do {
    line := ""
    every p := 1 to 8 do
      line ||:= s[n][2][p] || "%"
    write(filvar,line)}
  close(filvar)
end

procedure report()
  write("Space reserved for report.")
end

procedure get_version()
local filename,n
  n := 0
  write("Enter the name of the ORIGINAL filename ")
  filename := read()
  while close(open(filename[1:7] || (n +:= 1) || ".dat"))
return filename[1:7] || (n - 1) || ".dat"
end

procedure update()
local filename,filvar,n,student_list,line,student,
  inner_list,current
  filename := get_version()
  filvar := open(filename)
  student_list := []
  while line := read(filvar) do {
    student := students("","","",0,0,0,0,"")
    inner_list := list(2)
    n := 0
    line ?  while student[n +:= 1] := tab(upto("%")) do
      ="%"
    inner_list[1] := student.name
    inner_list[2] := student
    put(student_list,inner_list)}
  close(filvar)
  n := 0
```

```
  while current := student_list[n +:= 1][2] do {
    write("Name:  ",current.name)
    write("Current first exam = ",current.fstexam)
    writes("New score?  ")
    current.fstexam := read()
    write("Current second exam = ",current.secexam)
    writes("New score?  ")
    current.secexam := read()
    write("Current final exam = ",current.final)
    writes("New score?  ")
    current.final := read()
    student_list[n][2] := current}
  filename[7] +:= 1
  write_to_file(filename,student_list)
end
```

SUMMARY OF ICON FEATURES

1. A record is declared globally at the beginning of the program. It has a fixed number of fields which are named and may be accessed by creating a variable of this type and adding to its name a period and the field name.

2. A case statement allows for conditions with multiple choices. It tests the value of a variable and if it finds a match executes the statement following the colon after that match. A default condition may be included.

3. \t is the Icon character for a tab stop.

4. A substring of a string valued variable may be accessed by, for example, str[2:4] which produces the substring between positions 2 and 4 of str.

12
Conclusion

12.1 WORD PROCESSING

In this chapter we shall deal with a few items which may help you in your programming. Let us talk first a little about the question of word processing. This has become a major use of computers, even though it was a by-product of computing. Computing was originally intended to perform complex mathematical operations accurately and speedily, hence its name. The fact that letters of the alphabet and other symbols can be encoded as numbers made it possible for computers to manipulate texts as well as mathematical entities. Just half a century ago the word *computer* referred to a human being, and when the French came to need a word for the modern meaning of computer, they selected one which means *that which puts in order*, which is a better representation of the capabilities of the computer. There are many commercial word processors available, some of them inexpensive or even free, and it is not likely that you will want to compete with these products by writing your own program for word processing. However, it may occasionally be convenient to write a small program to perform some task that might be troublesome on your word processor. The SNOBOL-4 language became famous for its "one-line programs" which could do a limited task expeditiously, and Icon has similar capabilities. This is largely due to the fact that statements in Icon can "fail," which is equivalent to building in a condition into the statement; if certain circumstances prevail then the statement succeeds, and if they do not, it fails. This can be exploited to write very concise mini-programs. For example, let us say you have a file which uses the British spelling *colour*, and you wish to change it to the American usage which omits the *u*. In all probability your word processor will have a command to make such a change

133

throughout the file easily. But say you have a group of files that need such a change, and they have a set of related names such as file1, file2, and so on. In such a case it might be easier to write a little program to handle the change throughout. Let's consider the change in the spelling of the word first, assuming that we have a line in which the word occurs twice. The following loop will take care of it:

```
while line[find("colour",line) + 4] := ""
```

The inner function **find()** will look for the string we wish to change in the line. Since we are not using here the Icon scanning facility, the function requires as its second argument the string (in this case represented by the variable **line**) which is being searched. When we use Icon's scanning facility we do not need to do this, since the target string is cited right at the beginning prior to the question mark which initiates this facility. If **find()** succeeds, it returns the position at the beginning of the word. Used by itself as the index of the variable, this number represents the first letter in the word. By adding four to whatever this number is, we zero in on the offending *u*, and by assigning to it a null string we effectively delete it. This loop will keep on going as long as it finds the word *colour* in the line. When it has changed all occurrences, it will fail. Note that this loop has no "body." All the work it needs to do is performed by the assignment which takes place in the control statement beginning with **while**. By enclosing this loop in another loop which reads in lines for processing, and reads them out modified if necessary, we cover the entire file:

```
while line := read(infile) do {
  while line[find("colour",line) + 4] := ""
  write(outfile,line)}
```

Now we enclose all of this in a loop which takes care of each file in turn. Assuming we have twenty files, it will look like this:

```
every n := 1 to 20 do {
  infile := open("file" || n)
  outfile := open("file" || n || ".new","w")
```

followed by the same loop as before and the closing of the current files before the outermost loop is recommenced. You will now have the original set of files, and a modified set of files which have appended the extension *.new* to their names. There is a certain safety feature here; the original files are opened for reading only and so will undergo no change. The modified file was initially created by adding the second argument to the **open()** function. When you are satisfied that all is as it should be, you can delete the original files using *rm*, or *del*, or whatever your operating system uses. Here is the complete program:

```
#Omits the "u" in "colour" in twenty files

procedure main()
  process()
end

procedure process()
local n,infile,outfile,line
  every n := 1 to 20 do {
    infile := open("file" || n)
    outfile := open("file" || n || ".new","w")
    while line := read(infile) do {
      while line[find("colour",line) + 4] := ""
      write(outfile,line)}
    close(infile)
    close(outfile)}
end
```

Let us take another similar example. I have a set of files in which the names of the section headings are on a separate line and follow an indicator $\backslash section\{$, prescribed by the typesetting program, and each section heading is itself closed with a right curly bracket. I have each of these in small letters and wish to capitalize them all. The following line will achieve this:

```
line := line[1:match("\section{",line)] ||
  map(line[10:0],&lcase,&ucase)
```

In this instance the function match() is used. This function resembles find(), but it always starts at the beginning of the line, or if the scanning facility is being used, from the position of the imaginary pointer which may be moved up by tab() or move(). Additionally it returns the position after, rather than before, the string which is found. Obviously the position before would be uninteresting since we know where we are starting. We now give a range, from the first position through the end of what match() finds for us, and then concatenate it with the rest of the line (indicated by line[10:0]) after it has had all its small letters made capitals by using the map() function. The first argument is the string with which we are concerned, and all letters of the second argument which occur in the string are switched to the corresponding letters of the third argument, and returned as the value of the function. The values of the keywords representing the small and big letters are really sets, but are automatically switched to strings for this purpose by the Icon system, just as in selecting the filename it automatically changes the integers included in the filename to strings. These automatic changes of data type go on all the time in Icon, and save the programmer considerable effort. The opening and closing of the files can be handled in exactly the same way as before. Be sure that you have enough disk space to handle the new files you are creating.

Two questions arise with regard to these little programs. First, since they are so small why not simply put them into the main procedure? The answer is that procedures often get modified and reused, and it is better to start off with them as separate procedures, and use the main procedure only for traffic control. It is tempting to short-circuit by throwing everything into the main procedure, but this is a bad habit which should be avoided. Second, is it in order to use programs like this which contain no error checking? The answer is yes, provided that only you yourself use them, and you plan to use them promptly. It is a good idea to delete them after use, although you may want to save some procedures that look as if they could be reused. It would be inadvisable to allow someone else to use such a program. For example if there was already a file with the same name as the output file, this program would destroy that file in order to write the new one. It is easy to check to see if a file exists by attempting to open it and immediately close it. If that succeeds, then the file exists and you may warn the user that the file will be destroyed if the program is allowed to proceed. It is essential to put in such precautions against a careless user, since the risk of losing important information is a serious one. It also points out the need to back up files by making copies and placing them in some other location so that in the event of an accident all is not lost.

There is another potential use of Icon in connection with word processing. A new type of word processing program is a computerized typesetting program such as the LaTeX program used to produce this book. Such programs have commands written right into the text and these commands (which are distinguished in some way from regular text) ultimately instruct the printer how to act. It is possible to write an Icon template program which will, for instance, start a file with LaTeX commands to produce a letterhead, insert the date automatically from the calendar which your computer maintains, solicit interactively the name of the person you are addressing, and then read a file in which you have written a letter. It will then add the final salutation and the file will be complete to submit to the LaTeX program for processing. Here is a little piece of such a program which writes the date and the salutation:

```
write(outfile,"\\today"," \\\\[.25in]")
write("Enter the name to be placed be_
   tween Dear and the colon:")
name := read()
write(outfile, "Dear ",name,": \\\\[.25in]")
```

Assuming that the user responds with the name "John" to the prompt to enter a name, the resulting file represented by the variable outfile would look like this:

\today \\[.25in])
Dear John: \\[.25in])

and, assuming there was a previous command to use simulated typewriter type, the ultimate output will look like this:

August 27, 1989

Dear John:

Here the first line gives the order to print the current date, taken from the computer's internal calendar. The two backslashes and the measurement indicate a carriage return and a gap of a quarter of an inch. The second line writes *Dear John:* and again leaves a vertical space of a quarter of an inch. Unfortunately it is not possible to teach the LaTeX system here; for that you must consult Leslie Lamport's book LaTeX: *A Document Preparation System*. But it should enable you to get the general idea.

One word of caution. Many word processors do not limit themselves to the usual printing characters contained in the first 128 ASCII characters, but throw in additional characters for their own mode of processing. Be careful with such files, since manipulating them carelessly may interfere with the way in which they are handled by the particular word processor.

12.2 OTHER ICON FEATURES

Icon is a language rich in features, and those described in this book represent only a part of the capabilities of the language which are described in full in the Griswolds' book mentioned in Chapter 1, along with the supplementary paper referred to there. The features discussed so far make possible programs of considerable complexity. Here some additional features will be discussed which are less likely to be used regularly but may prove useful from time to time.

12.3 CO-EXPRESSIONS

Certain expressions known as generators produce a sequence of results rather than a single result. For example, 1 to 10 produces the first ten digits in sequence. We have used this generator with the **every** loop to cause a loop to function a fixed number of times. It is possible to feed such a sequence into a variable, and produce the next number in the sequence whenever we wish. For example, consider the following fragment of code which would produce a "menu," and store the user's response in the variable **answer**:

```
write("Would you like to:")
write("1.  Initialize")
write("2.  Update")
write("3.  Report")
writes("Enter number selected:   ")
answer := read()
```

If, as the program develops, we change the order of the items in the menu, or insert new ones, we shall constantly be changing the numbers. We could avoid that by rewriting the program fragment as follows:

```
a := create 1 to 10
write("Would you like to:")
write(@a,".  Initialize")
write(@a,".  Update")
write(@a,".  Report")
writes("Enter number selected:   ")
answer := read()
```

The first line stores the result sequence of 1 to 10 in the variable a, and every time we write that variable preceded by the at-sign, the next result of the sequence is produced. This is known as a co-expression. In this way, the numbering will always be correct, provided it does not exceed 10, however much we change around the items, or insert new ones.

Additionally, we can reset the sequence to the beginning by prefixing a circumflex to the variable containing the result sequence.

```
b := ^a
```

stores in b the whole sequence anew from the beginning. The keyword &current contains the current co-expression, and may be useful if you are using several.

12.4   FILE HANDLING

We have already learned to use the function **open()** which gets a file ready to use if it already exists, and creates it first if it does not. Files should always be closed with **close()** as soon as they are no longer needed. A file can be deleted from within a program by using the function **remove()**. The sole argument to this function is the *name* of the file (not a file variable.) The file should always be closed before it is deleted. This function should be used with caution, since it is possible to delete files later using the operating system. If you are working under MS-DOS, you must use a version of Icon which includes functions like this which access the operating system. The archived version in which Icon is supplied for MS-DOS contains versions with

and without this facility. See Appendix D for details. In order to extract the
version of Icon which includes access to the operating system, instead of the
command

  a:arc x a:ficonx.arc ficonx.exe

mentioned there, use the following:

  a:arc x a:ficonx.arc ficonxp.exe

You can then change the name of the extracted file to iconx.exe and use it
just like the version which does not access the operating system. In order to
avoid confusion, you can do one of several things:

- Keep the new file on a separate disk, and mark it as the disk with the
  form of Icon which has access to the operating system. Of course, you
  will need the other files that constitute the rest of the Icon system.

- Keep the new file in a different directory. If you do not understand
  the directory system, refer to the chapter on *Directory Features* in your
  computer manual.

- Retain the name *ficonxp.exe*. You will then have to execute programs
  using *ficonxp* rather than the usual *iconx*. However, in this case you will
  not be able to translate and execute programs immediately by using the
  -*x* addition.

Another function can be used to give a file a new name. This is **rename()**
which takes two arguments, separated as usual by commas, the first of which
is the current name of the file, and the second is the new name.

As an example of how we might use these two functions, let us revert to
those twenty files we spoke about earlier in this chapter in which we changed
"colour" to "color". After concluding the changes, and perhaps arranging for
some check that all is as it should be, we might delete the old files containing
"colour", and then give the new file the original name:

```
every n := 1 to 20 do {
  remove("file" || n)
  rename("file" || n || ".new","file" || n)}
```

Finally, the MS-DOS version of Icon has several words which refer to
"files" which are really peripheral parts of the computer system, or no file at
all. PRN refers to the printer, so using it as the first argument to a **write()**
statement will have the subsequent arguments printed on the printer rather
than being inscribed on a disk file, provided that a printer is properly attached
to the computer. Similarly CON refers to the console (the keyboard), AUX

refers to the auxiliary port which enables other gadgets to be attached, and NUL refers to no file, i.e., anything sent there falls into a black hole and disappears, but no errors are generated. These may be useful if you want to send your output elsewhere than to the screen or a disk file, which are the most usual targets.

A
Computer Character Sets

Computer character sets are an inheritance from telegraphy (Greek: *writing from a distance*) and a little history will aid in their understanding. In the sixteenth century the Italian physician and mathematician Gerolamo Cardano (1501-1576) suggested that messages could be sent by lighting beacons on five towers. If we designate an unlighted tower by 0 and a lighted tower by 1, then we can have a code such as:

00001	(beacon 5 lighted)	=	A
00010	(beacon 4 lighted)	=	B
00011	(beacons 4 & 5 lighted)	=	C

There are 32 possible combinations(2^5) and this allows for the entire alphabet plus a few extra characters. Cardano had in effect discovered the *bit* or binary digit, i.e., a unit of information which can have one of two states (lighted/unlighted, 0/1, strong current/weak current, and so on.) By combining these bits, messages can be encoded. Systems of lanterns using Cardano's principle became common in the nineteenth century. The five-bit Baudot Code named after the French engineer and inventor Jean-Maurice-Émile Baudot (1845-1903) was widely used in the transmission of messages by electrical means. Some characters were used to give information or instructions to the teletype at the other end of the line (to return the carriage or to indicate the end of the message, for example). These had no graphic representation and came to be known as *control characters*. In 1966 the American Standard Code for Information Interchange known as *ASCII* was adopted. This uses seven bits for information and hence has $2^7 = 128$ possible combinations.

141

There is an extra bit used for checking the accuracy of the transmission, and this makes a total of eight bits. In the ASCII code the first thirty-two characters (from 0 to 31) are control characters; for example, number 12 was used to instruct the machine to eject a page, and so was known as *formfeed* or *FF*. Now *L* in the ASCII code is character 76 which in eight binary digits is 01001100. Character 12 in binary digits is 00001100. To send character 12 the machine simply changed the second digit of character 76 from 1 to 0, and hence this is called control-L. (The "second digit" is normally called bit 6, starting from zero and numbering from the right—which betrays the Semitic origin of our numerical notation system!) The operator indicates this to the machine by pressing *L* while holding down the control key. (Lowercase letters bear a similar relationship. They change the third digit to a 1—01101100.) It is interesting to observe that the highest character 127 is also a control character called *rubout* or *delete*. This is on account of the paper tape which was widely used for input. Once a tape has holes in it (indicating *1*'s) it is impossible to remove them. But it was possible to backspace and then make all seven digits *1*'s by punching all of them, since repunching a hole leaves it unchanged. Hence the character 127 (01111111 in binary) was simply ignored. In adapting to computers, many of the control characters lost their original meaning and are used arbitrarily for a number of purposes (especially in word processing) although some of them such as *control-C* for *end of text* remain in many applications. Thus in the WORD∗STAR word processing program *control-D* means "advance the cursor one character" while in the EMACS editor it means "delete the character at the cursor." Such decisions are made by the author of the particular program, and there is little consistency between different programs. A control character is often indicated by placing a wedge or caret (∧ or ^) in front of the normal printing character. In Icon this notation may be used to represent control characters if preceded by a backslash. The backslash indicates the special nature of the wedge. Thus in a string \^L represents *control-L*. Since the additional bit which was used for checking the correctness of the transmission may not be required in computer usage, this extra bit can also be used to represent characters, and the extended ASCII set of 256 characters contains additional symbols such as letters with accents used in foreign languages and mathematical characters. There are other character sets, for example EBCDIC which also has 256 characters but in a quite different order from ASCII, and some special character sets for scientific applications. ASCII is now widely used however.

It is worthwhile mentioning one matter which is the result of historical developments. The typewriter moved to a new line by two distinct movements. First, the carriage shifted to the beginning of the line. Then the platten moved sufficiently to feed in enough paper for one line. For this purpose the character set had two control characters: one to return the carriage and one to perform a linefeed. On computer screens which have no carriage, only one character is needed. This is therefore dubbed "newline" and just the linefeed character is used. Icon represents this by \l (for "linefeed" and \n (for "newline"). These are the same character (ASCII 10). Icon uses \r for the carriage return character (ASCII 13). This will cause the cursor to return to the beginning of the line.

B
Custom-Designed Character Sets

It is possible to have a custom-designed alphabet to use on the screen of your personal computer using MS-DOS, and this appendix suggests a way in which it can be done. While the procedure is somewhat tedious, it needs only to be done once, and then you can use your Armenian or Ukrainian character set in your programs whenever you want. This has been successfully implemented on the Zenith microcomputer using the MS-DOS operating system. You should be aware that some computers handle their graphic screen differently, and it may not work on such computers. Unfortunately "compatibility" between different computers is not always as easy as it looks.

First, you should ensure that you have the following MS-DOS files on the disk with which you boot your computer. If they are on another disk they should be copied onto the disk you are using, and be sure that you have some room left over by removing some files you do not need if necessary. They are:

- ANSI.SYS

- GRAFTABL.COM

- DEBUG.COM

Then go through the following steps.

1. Create a file called CONFIG.SYS with EDLIN or some other editor and include in it the command

    DEVICE=ANSI.SYS

This will enable you to use the character set you create on the graphic screen. If you are already using the file CONFIG.SYS with some other instructions, simply add this command on a new line following those already there.

2. Create the characters you wish to use on an 8×8 grid leaving each square blank, or blacking it in. You can use graph paper for this purpose. Leave one row at the top or bottom and one column on one side blank to allow for space between the letters.

3. Convert each grid to a numerical value as follows. Starting with the top horizontal row, call each blank square 0 and each penciled in square 1. So if the row has the first and sixth column blackened it will be represented by 10000100. Convert this binary number to a hex[1] number by taking the first four digits and then the second four and converting them in accordance with the following:

0000 = 0	0001 = 1	0010 = 2	0011 = 3	0100 = 4
0101 = 5	0110 = 6	0111 = 7	1000 = 8	1001 = 9
1010 = A	1011 = B	1100 = C	1101 = D	1110 = E
1111 = F				

For example, a row that was originally 10000100 becomes 84. Each 8×8 grid will then be represented by 8 numbers. So the Hebrew letter *aleph* may be represented by

00 22 12 1A 2C 24 22 00

4. Make a copy of GRAFTABL.COM under a different name thus:

COPY GRAFTABL.COM NEWTABL.COM <return>

This will create a copy of GRAFTABL.COM which we shall modify.

5. Type in

DEBUG NEWTABL.COM <return>

You should see a "prompt" consisting of a dash (−). Type in

E0DF1:103 00 22 12 1A 2C 24 22 00 <return>

---

[1] *Hex* stands for *hexadecimal* and refers to the system using sixteen rather than ten as the base. In this system the regular numerals are supplemented by the first six letters of the alphabet to represent decimal 10–15.

(Of course, the eight pairs of hex digits will be whatever you want them to be.) To enter the next one type

E0DF1:10B

followed by eight hex pairs and <return>.

You must constantly increment the hex number after the colon by 8, but you must use hex arithmetic. If you like, DEBUG will do the hex arithmetic for you; enter

H 10B 8

and it will give the result of adding and subtracting 10B and 8. (You want the addition of course.) When you have finished, type in W (for *write*) and hit return. Your disk file will be saved as you modified it. Type in Q to quit DEBUG. Then reboot, type in NEWTABL <return>, and your characters are ready to use. The graphic screen on which you can use them is activated by the command

write("\e[=5h")

provided that you have set up the CONFIG.SYS file as just detailed.

The Icon function **char(n)** where **n** is a number between 128 and 255 included in your programs will return one of the characters you have created. You may create a maximum of 128 characters in this manner. To restore the regular screen the command is

write("\e[=2h")

The use of color and the hi-res screen is also possible. You may consult documentation of the ANSI.SYS terminal driver for further information.

C
The EDLIN Editor

This appendix gives some additional information on using EDLIN. First, a useful feature in line editing. We mentioned in the text that the forward arrow or F1 may be used to reproduce a letter from the line being edited. You may speed up this process by pressing F2 and a single letter. It will then reproduce the letters from the line up to the letter that was entered. F4 will delete letters in a similar fashion, but should be used with caution!

You may delete lines by entering the number of the first line to be deleted followed by a comma and the number of the second line to be deleted followed by *d*. If you enter only one number, it will delete that one line.

If you wish to replace a single word, the easiest way is to use the line editing feature by entering the line number, using F1 or F2 to reach the item you wish to change, entering the new item, and using F3 to complete the line. However, if you wish to change the same word over several lines of text, you may enter the number of the first line in which you wish the change to be made followed by a comma and the number of the last number. Then enter *r* (for "replace") and the string you wish to replace. Then press the F6 key, enter the new string, and press return. If you insert a question mark before the *r* you will be queried before each change, which makes selective changes possible. In this way you could prevent the change of the substring embedded in another word. Sometimes one may decide to change the name of a variable, and then this command is quite useful.

It is possible to search the file or part of it for a particular string. This is done by entering the range of lines as for the "replace" command, the letter *s* (for "search"), the string that is being sought, and return. This will find the first occurrence of the string. If you type a question mark before the *s*, you will be queried if that is the string you are looking for, and if you respond

149

with n, the search will be continued.

The line currently being edited is marked by EDLIN with an asterisk, and can be referred to by using a period instead of the line number; however, it is probably safer to use the line number. The pound sign can similarly be used to indicate the number after the last line in the file, so if you want to add new lines to the file you may use this. Actually any number higher than the number of lines in the file would do.

EDLIN works by taking the file it is editing into memory. If there is not room for the whole file, it takes part of it. EDLIN informs you if it has been able to bring the entire file into memory, but otherwise you must assume that only part is available for editing. When you have edited this part, you may use the command w to write edited lines to the file, and thereby make room for new lines to edit. You can then use the command a to append new lines to the section you are editing.

D
Some Hints on Running Icon Programs

If you are using a time-sharing system, you may use the command *icont* followed by the name of a file bearing the extension *.icn* and containing Icon code. You may omit the extension if you wish. This invokes the Icon translator which converts your code into a form that the Icon system can run. This is placed in a file of the same name but with no extension or on some systems with the extension *icx*. You can then run your program by typing in the filename without the extension. In some cases you must precede it by the command *iconx*. It is possible to combine both these steps by adding *-x* at the end of the line that invokes the translator. This will run the program as soon as it is translated. Normally, however, it is not a good idea to do this, because there will probably be some errors in your code, and the Icon system will tell you where these occurred and offer some hints as to what may be wrong. So you will not want to run the program until you are sure any errors have been removed. If Icon is not yet on your system you may want to ask your system manager to install it; it can be obtained at nominal cost.

If you are using a microcomputer, you will need at least 512K of memory in order to run Icon. You must have available the following files which together constitute the Icon system:

- icont.exe

- itran.exe

- ilink.exe

- iconx.exe

151

The easiest way for a beginner to obtain these is probably to copy them from a friend. They are all in the public domain, and may be copied without cost or formality provided that they are not changed in any way. Otherwise you may obtain the files for a modest fee from commercial outlets or the Icon project at the University of Arizona. In this case, you may receive the files in an archived condition which makes it possible to compress them onto a small number of disks. If you receive the files in an archived condition, you must extract them from the archive. Proceed as follows. Boot up your computer with the system disk. Place a blank, formatted disk in drive B. If you do not know how to format a disk, follow the instructions in your computer manual. You may have to check the word *format* in the index to find the instructions. Place the disk containing the archive in disk drive A. Type in the command *dir* in order to see what is on the disk. You need to have there a file ARC.EXE which will enable you to extract the files you need. Then look for the files TRANLINK.ARC and FICONX.ARC which contain the files you need. Type in *B:* and hit the return key. This will make your B drive the one you are working with. Then enter

   a:arc x a:tranlink.arc

and hit return. This should place on the disk in drive B several files which you need to operate the Icon system. Then enter

   a:arc x a:ficonx.arc ficonx.exe

and hit return. This will place on drive B another file you need. You must then change the name of this file as follows:

   rename ficonx.exe iconx.exe

The reason for this is that this is the file containing that part of the Icon system which actually runs your program, and you have several options for this file of which we have extracted one only. Any of them should have the name *iconx.exe* when you run the programs, so you have to see that it is named correctly.

   It may be that these archived files are themselves included in archive and so you will not see the names I have mentioned. In this case, type in

   a:arc x a:

followed immediately by the name of the file that you find there. This will remove the hidden files from their archive. You will not need the remainder of the information in this appendix until you have had some experience using Icon, and wish to speed up your development of programs.

Translation may be slow on microcomputers, since a great deal of disk access is involved. This procedure can be substantially speeded up by using a "virtual disk," assuming that your computer has sufficient available memory. This involves running a program (for example MSDOS's *VDISK*) which sets aside part of the memory which it treats as though it were a disk. The files of the Icon system can then be copied on to this virtual disk at the beginning of the session, and this will be found to greatly speed up program development. It is important to back up any files newly created in this way on to a "real" disk, since the virtual disk ceases to exist when power is no longer supplied to the computer. *VDISK* is installed by including the command

DEVICE=VDISK.SYS 256

in the CONFIG.SYS file which is explained in Section 6.2. This will devote one-half of the memory of a 512K computer for this purpose. VDISK takes to itself the next available drive letter, so on a system with two floppy disk drives, the "disk" will be designated as *C:*. This will give you room to develop your translated file. But you probably will have to execute your programs without the benefit of a virtual disk unless you have more than 512K of memory.

Another way to speed program development is to pretranslate commonly used procedures. Thus, we might place **procedure getword()** on a file called **getw.icn**. We then enter

icont -c getw.icn

This produces two files, *getw.u1* and *getw.u2*. Then if we have a file containing an Icon program called *proj7.icn*, we may use the procedure in the course of the program without including the body of the procedure. We do this by including at the beginning of our program in the file *proj7.icn* the declaration

link getw

The files *getw.u1* and *getw.u2* must be present. The resultant file *proj7* will then have the getword procedure linked to it and will execute correctly. This also saves translation time and avoids the necessity of repeating commonly used procedures in the source code. You may link several such files, and they will be separated by commas in the link declaration.

Index